Hockey Training for Kids

# HOCKEY
## TRAINING FOR KIDS

**ZDENEK PAVLIS**

MEYER & MEYER SPORT

Original Titel: Příručka Pro Trenéry Ledního Hokeje
II. Část
© Zdeněk Pavliš, 2000

British Library Cataloguing in Publication Data
A catalogue record for this book is available from the British Library

Hockey Training for Kids
Oxford: Meyer & Meyer Sport (UK) Ltd., 2007
ISBN 10: 1-84126-194-7
ISBN 13: 978-1-84126-194-2

© 2007 by Meyer & Meyer Sport (UK) Ltd.
Aachen, Adelaide, Auckland, Budapest, Graz, Johannesburg,
New York, Olten (CH), Oxford, Singapore, Toronto
Member of the World
Sports Publishers' Association (WSPA)
www.w-s-p-a.org
Printed and bound by: B.O.S.S Druck und Medien GmbH, Kleve
ISBN 10: 1-84126-194-7
ISBN 13: 978-1-84126-194-2
E-Mail: verlag@m-m-sports.com
www.m-m-sports.com

# CONTENTS

**Foreword**

**T**his book follows on from the first two titles in the series (**"Hockey – The Basics"** and **"Hockey – First Steps for Kids"**) and covers mainly player skills. Trainers will also find in this series several important tips (for example **Training Examples, The Organization of Training and Managing Training**), which is a 'must-have' for his practical work.

The main element of this book deals with nine and ten year olds. Because of systematic reasons, however, several themes and skills are covered, which players in this age group will not all have mastered yet. Therefore, the material covered is not only valid for this age category.

The book describes the different age and phases of a child's development in relation to the motor system of the young player. The framework plans recommended for hockey skills for each of the age groups are laid out as per the system of ice hockey. The book covers the technique and methods of all individual attack and defense actions very comprehensively, and numerous game combinations are suggested. The problems of being able to do the face-off are often underestimated both in specialist publications as well as in practice. The problems are often only considered from a tactical viewpoint.

Because of the individual training practice and with the cooperation of a few excellent players, the main element covers not only the training methods but also the commonest face-off techniques in all zones of the ice. Besides this, the book includes numerous examples of complete training sessions and over 100 ice hockey exercises. The book provides suggestions to the trainer for creative and successful work with his young ice hockey players.

*Zdeněk Pavliš*

# 1

# The Main Aims of Training

The age of a 9-10 year old seems to be the best phase for learning new movement skills (sometimes it is called the "golden age of the motor system"). It is therefore necessary to make best use of this age group, and this means not only on the ice but also in training off the ice rink. Above all, however, having fun and enjoyment playing ice hockey must always be the main thing that is to be highly rated.

During the further training of this age group, the following aims and exercises form the main emphasis for young ice hockey players.

■ The development of a variety of basic movement skills, while at the same time taking the specific phases in the development of the young body and organism into consideration. In general training sessions, the movement skills already learned should be expanded upon.

■ When training on the ice it is also important to learn as many new movement skills as possible (with two main emphases in mind – skating and puck control).

■ To master the technical and tactical basics of ice hockey (combinations, basics of teamwork).

■ To develop a solid understanding of the systematic training for ice hockey.

■ To be able to explain terms such as "Training", "Daily routine" and "Regeneration".

■ To master a basic knowledge and the basics of the graphic symbols used in ice hockey.

■ To get to know the rules of ice hockey better.

■ To learn to accept the word of the opponent, the referees, trainers and assistants and to provide support to children in learning respect and honesty.

■ To develop communication and interhuman relations in children further.

■ To build up a positive relationship to the sporting traditions of the sports club, the town and to the former players in the club.

# Differences in Age and Development

The age of 9-10 years old is the period of a child's young school age and this can be divided into two further, relatively separate periods – childhood and pre-puberty or otherwise classed as childhood and later childhood.

This age is also characterized generally as the period of the development of the motor senses. Children develop in many different ways. They are optimistic and interest themselves in all sorts of things. Where their energy can be properly harnessed, they are easily led along. Movement activity is all about having enjoyment and fun and they do not need to be pushed to take on activities. They like competitive games where the game itself is the reason for doing it at all.

## Physical Development

Physical development is characterized by a steady increase in height and weight. They gain about 2-3 inches in height each year. At the same time, of course, the inner organs, blood circulation and the lungs develop and the amount of energy increases. The spine becomes stronger, the hardening of the bones increases in pace and despite this the joints remain supple and elastic. The morphology of the body begins to change and its biological mechanics with it, so that the relativity between the trunk and the extremities are given better conditions to develop further movement actions.

The development of the brain (the brain as the main organ of the central nerve system) was complete prior to the beginning of this period. Although some nerve structures still have to mature, there is still room for the development of new, random reflexes to be able to execute complicated coordination movements and the development of speed.

## Psychological Development

The gain in knowledge in this period is enormous. Parallel to this the memory and imaginative capacity is being developed. The child's thought process concentrates now more on the details rather than the context. The increase in sensitivity of the environment, however, can have a disturbing effect.

The ability to understand abstract terms is not yet sufficiently developed. The brain is mainly busy with reality, with the features of objects and actual events. The ability to think abstractly comes first of all at the end of this period.

Behavior is still quite unstable. Children are impulsive and quickly switch between good and bad moods. Willpower has not yet been properly developed and a child does not manage to follow an aim for long where it has maybe to overcome failures. The child experiences most activities with intense feelings and it is particularly aware of its environment. A sense of team spirit has already been developed and the children work together willingly. They begin to understand the rules. The capacity to exercise self-criticism is still not yet fully developed.

## Development of Movement

Considering the development of movement, much typical spontaneity can be seen in the activities of this age group. New movement skills are quickly learned, but if they are not repeated often then they are just as quickly forgotten. When learning new skills, normal experiences from practicing movements are used as background. The child is in the "golden age of the development of the motor system".

Indeed, the 10-year-old is at the best optimum age for the development of the motor activities. Confidence in executing the activities increases and in the movements, all the characteristics of a correct performance can be observed. The children are already in a position to be able to carry out strenuous coordination exercises and achieve difficult movement structures.

## Social Development

A period of critical social development begins at this age and this manifests itself in expressions of judgement about what is happening (at school, in the family and also in the sports club). The children often judge these things negatively and sometimes, as a result of this, the parental authority, and that of grown-ups, can be seen to drop away. The child seeks a role model that it finds eventually amongst his pals, who represent a natural authority to the child. The child begins to adopt cultural basic habits that increase its ability to integrate and socialize (finding its feet in new groups). Gradually the child begins to take on responsibility for its own actions.

# 3
# The Development
# of Movement Ability

T
he term movement ability is understood as being the relatively independent grouping of internal prerequisites of the human organism to execute a movement activity. In the main, this concerns inborn movement prerequisites that one does not learn but rather ones that can be so to speak developed more or less. To develop them requires long-term training.

## Important points for movement ability:
**a)** Speed,
**b)** Agility (some authors speak of the ability to coordinate),
**c)** Strength,
**d)** Stamina and
**e)** Flexibility.

> ### Note:
> *There is a difference between movement ability and movement skills. Skills are understood as being learned prerequisites for the correct, quick and effective execution of a movement task (doing a roll, skating, shooting the puck etc.).*

The age between 6 and 14 years old is particularly important for the quality of the development of individual movement abilities. Therefore, the young player should be trained in as many of the basics as possible, on which successful training can then be progressed. Training must include all the abilities without neglecting one or the other.

The main emphasis in the development of the individual movement abilities in this age group takes place, above all, off the ice rink. Therefore, it is recommended that during the main part of the training period (competition period) practice is done at least once a week (preferably twice a week) on firm ground. The aim of this training session is the development of agility in combination with speed, strength and flexibility (gymnastics, hurdling, different ball games).

The training session on the ice, on the other hand, serves to develop and improve movement skills such as skating, dribbling with the puck, shooting techniques, passing and receiving passes, and should not be conceived as fitness training for the young players. After learning the movement techniques, speed and coordination ability is brought to the fore in the training on the ice (of course with a simultaneous development of flexibility).

With the requirement to observe regularity in the development of the human organism, this is also connected to the various phases of development of the motor system. In certain age phases there are more suitable conditions prevailing for the development of a particular movement ability than in other phases of the age group.

The age between 9 and 10 years old is particularly suitable for the development of agility, as well as the majority of the interrelated abilities – principally a feeling for balance and the development of speed (above all reaction and pace). With the gradual development of strength, speed training becomes a possibility. Sprinting exercises are suitable but always with an eye on making sure that the exercises fit the age group in this category. In certain phases of development a variety of training effectiveness in the individual movement abilities will be achieved.

### Training effectiveness is:
**a]** high
- for 7-10 year olds when combining movements.
- for 8-13 year olds when concentrating on the feeling of balance.

**b]** in medium range
- for 7-10 year olds when concentrating on correcting rapid reactions.
- for 7-10 year olds when doing sprinting training (speed).
- for 7-10 year olds in their agility.

A characteristic feature of the category for 9-10 year olds is training variety outside the ice stadium. The development of the coordination and feeling of balance is carried out using simple gymnastics and rhythm exercises, running exercises, various ball games, hurdling and above all hand, eye, leg and trunk coordination exercises. Basic exercises are speed sprinting, agility, coordination, stretching and balance exercises. Training should be intense and coupled with sufficient regeneration timeouts.

In this age group, it seems that the best form of exercises for the later development of strength are the ones covering technique and balance training. These exercises are carried out using only light wooden poles (ice hockey sticks). Besides the schooling of the technique and balance, the suppleness of the joints is improved at the same time.

For this age category, long periods of strain are not suitable. Training, using a variety of playing exercises is more appropriate. At the beginning of training sessions, stretching exercises should be done and at the end of training simple gymnastics with strengthening, agility and the often-neglected breathing exercises should round off the session.

The following table shows the percentage of time that should be devoted to the development of the individual movement abilities:

| Age Group | Speed | Agility | Strength | Stamina | Game Play |
|-----------|-------|---------|----------|---------|-----------|
| 9-10 years | 20% | 20% | 10% | 10% | 40% |

## al  Speed

Speed is one of the basic abilities in child and youth ice hockey training. This means short and brief periods of movement (3-15 seconds) carried out at high intensity. However, this length of time appears to be too long for ice hockey. Here we speak of periods of 3-10 seconds, while the other intensity parameters stay the same. When carrying out speed training, different actions should be included for the various parts of the body – arms, rear, legs etc.

When doing speed training, the following intensity parameters apply:
- Total time: 3-15 seconds (however, better with 3-10 seconds).
- Intensity: Maximum.
- Number of repeats: 2-6 per set; 2-3 sets.
- Recovery time: 2-3 minutes when training off the ice, on the ice in proportion 1: 8, between individual sets 5-8 minutes with active workout.

For 9-10 year old players, the main emphasis is on the development of speed off the ice (on a pitch, in the gymnasium). This ability, however, is not often trained on the ice. Speed exercises should be first attempted once the correct technique has been mastered. The exercises should only last 3-7 seconds and they are carried out without an opposing player and in simple conditions (starts, skating forwards also with bump stops etc.).

## Training off the ice

- Running exercises (up to 30 m).
- Various games – catching games.
- Relays.
- Sports games.
- Sprints.
- Hurdling.
- Slalom runs.
- Running with rapid changes of direction – forwards, backwards, sideways (important).
- Reaction exercises – with a start signal – starts from various positions, slalom, hill climbs etc., with all the possible variations – speed of reaction, orientation, anticipation etc.

## Training on the ice

- Simple, individual game actions and team play at maximum speed (after mastering the techniques).
- Various ice-skating routines with changes of direction (at maximum speed).
- Special speed training at least once a week (starts, sprints up to 3 m, bump stops, rapid changes of direction etc.).
- Inclusion of certain variations of speed training in each training session.
- Short periods of game play at maximum speed.

In cases where the aim of training (whether on the ice or off) is not to develop speed, each training session nevertheless includes several speed exercises. These are simple exercises lasting only 3-7 seconds to be repeated 2-4 times proportionally at a rate of 1:8 (off the ice 1:10 or 2-3 minutes). Exercises like these should be repeated only 2-3 times during the whole training session (dependent on the type of training and its content).

## b] Agility

There are specific principles used when developing the ability of agility:

a] Prefer to select demanding, coordination exercises that have an increasing degree of difficulty (cartwheel – handspring – somersault).

b] Carry out the exercises doing different variations (change of rhythm, changes made following audible or optical signals).

c] Carry out the exercises in changing external conditions (e.g., downhill and uphill runs, running in water, in sand etc.).

d] Combine movement skills already learned one after the other quickly (e.g., acrobatic exercises – forward roll – jump up – turn round – backward roll).

e] Combine several exercises with each other (e.g., with two balls – dribbling with one of the balls, while throwing the other up in the air – do a volleyball smash then sit down and stand up).

f] Carry out exercises that have been learned in non-standard variations (scrabble backwards on all fours, doing a roll with a partner etc.).

g] Doing exercises against the clock (maximum speed, with the requirement to make split decisions, with limitations on time and space – e.g., training in pairs do 10 headstands in 10 seconds, Situation 1:1 on the left-hand side of the pitch, without being allowed to dodge to the right).

h] Instruction for the exercise given first of all during its execution – dribbling the puck and jumping over a hurdle – the trainer says in which direction the puck must be passed first after the player has started to jump etc.

Recommended, suitable exercise variations include all forms of agility exercises, acrobatic exercises, exercises with a ball, orientation games (trampoline jumping), gymnastics with the horse, playing little games etc. Agility can be combined with speed training very easily (e.g., relay races, hurdling).

### Training off the ice

- Various games (soccer, football, rugby, field hockey, other little games etc.).
- Gymnastics (acrobatics on the mat, on the trampoline, gym equipment – take safety precautions).
- Orientation exercises.
- Balancing exercises – walking, running, jumps with turns and changes of direction, exercises on gym benches, exercises with a rope.
- Agility exercises in water, jumping and diving into water.

- Clearing different heights of hurdle.
- Various running variations with rapid changes of direction (slalom in a straight line and round a circle).

### Training on the ice

- Playing games in narrow spaces.
- Little games.
- Various ice-skating routines with changes of direction, dodging opposition, kneeling down, doing turns, falling down and doing a roll forwards standing up quickly afterwards – with and without the puck.
- Individual, difficult game play actions (e.g., shooting on the turn).
- Coordination exercises.

## c] Strength

For this age group strength ability is only considered as a support for the development of speed and agility. Generally, exercises using bursts of strength to train the legs and speed training are done in conjunction with coordination exercises. In young players (up to about 12 years old), due to low hormone production, it is recommended that strength is developed using the circling method in training with the following main emphasis:

- Martial arts.
- Exercises under difficult conditions – running in water, in sad, carrying a partner, running uphill etc.
- Explosive strength – little games, jumping and plunging exercises, throwing training.
- Strength training using the body weight – press-ups, chin-ups, climbing, using gym equipment.
- Exercising with small hand weights (0,5-1,5 kg) and with low weight medicine balls.
- On the ice – tackling, continuous shooting at goal, skating (also against some form of resistance – e.g., pushing or pulling a partner).

So-called **strengthening blocks** have proved to give good results. The term strengthening blocks is understood as being breaks in training, in which strengthening exercises are done (for example a break in training when five press-ups and five jump-ups are done).

For young players, the main emphasis in strength training is on the large muscle parts of the body (stomach, back, thighs, shoulders etc.). All the exercises should be done in a playful manner avoiding any great strain on the spine. After finishing each set of exercises, the part of the body that has been exercised must be 'stretched' and regenerative and breathing exercises done as well.

## d] Stamina

Generally, stamina in children is already at a limit of natural development. This means that at this age, stamina cannot be improved in any considerable amount. The reason for this lies in the physiological nature, which limits the burning up of oxygen in a young player.

From a viewpoint of using methods, interval training cannot be recommended, because this method induces higher rates of the production of lactates. The alternate change method, however, is suitable being based on a continuous load with a pulse rate intensity of 170-175 per minute. Running falls well into this category. However, because of its monotonous character, this is not very popular with children. For the development of stamina, other variations of the alternate change method can be better used. One optimum possibility is the "Fartlek" method (Game played at speed).

### Example

*Running constantly at low to medium intensity, followed by quicker running bursts (competitions, relays), followed by a little game or strengthening exercises using the weight of your own body (tree climbing, variations of jumping actions, hurdling etc.). The whole exercise concerns a change over between low and high load intensity, not necessarily achieved only by running. Where the terrain permits, forward rolls, cartwheels to the side, turns followed by rapid starts in any direction can be incorporated. At the end (five minutes), this is followed by a cool down period of lower intensity exercises and loosening exercises. The whole program should last about 30-40 minutes.*

*The so-called play forms are also popular. The youngsters are not allowed to stand still when doing activities such as soccer, field hockey etc. If one of them happens to be standing about then he has to do a penalty e.g., a forward roll, a sideways cartwheel or a squatting jump up. This should guarantee the necessary load intensity. The changeovers should occur in longer intervals (2-3 minutes). The game form brings with it more than enough liveliness and emotion into the training.*

*As the main component for developing stamina on the ice, the game itself should suffice. Parallel to the training of the technical and tactical skills (individual game play actions, combinations), the intensity and the number of repeats will be achieved by observing the optimum length of the loading.*

*Training off the ice can be complemented by using all the cyclical types of sports and exercises (walking, running, swimming, cycling and steeplechasing).*

## e] Flexibilty

The development of flexibility is a very important part of training children. In ice hockey, one often experiences one-sided loading, which results in negative consequences later in body posture. Here we are talking about underdeveloped or weak muscles and even problems with the spine. Therefore, it is important that every training session contains stretching, regenerative and breathing exercises.

For the development of the ability to be flexible, from a viewpoint of methods, active, static stretching exercises are preferable. In children (9 and 10 years old) stretching must be done very carefully. The children are not yet able to recognize the limits they may go to when stretching (the pain threshold). Passive stretching exercises (with a partner) are not suitable, because at this age the joints and connective tissues can be relatively easily damaged.

## Methodical tips for the development of flexibility

- Exercises for flexibility are incorporated regularly into the whole of the annual training program.

- In the preparation period, a higher degree of flexibility should be developed.

- Flexibility is systematically and routinely developed. The young players should do the stretching exercises before and after the competitive games, individually in the mornings and in the changing rooms.

- In training, the stretching exercises are done mainly in the preparatory period after a full and complete warm-up session.

- Above all, in training, static stretching exercises are preferable and the passive ones only carried out with a lot of care.

- It is not advisable to try to develop flexibility when very tired (i.e., at the end of training or after a very exhausting session of stamina training etc.). Tip: Agility exercises should not be confused with loosening, regenerative and breathing exercises. These exercises are done at the end of the training.

- Make sure you maintain the principle of gradually increasing the loading and dynamics of flexibility.

- Each exercise is repeated 12-15 times combined with an adequate number of loosening exercises.

- Static exercises, done in the preparatory part of the training session, should last at least 10 minutes (providing that they are not one of the elements of the main flexibility sessions). At the end of training they should take 20-30 minutes with 2-3 repeats.

- Where any kind of pain is felt or there are unpleasant feelings in the muscles, the exercises must be stopped.

- After a stand down following an injury, the rate of loading should only be gradually increased.

- Flexibility exercises at the beginning and end are a firm part of every training session. Also they should be used for every strength training session.

- At the end of each training session, regenerative (exercises to maintain a correct body posture) and breathing exercises should never be forgotten.

# Methodical Tips for the Further Training Sessions

**D**uring the annual cycle, for training off the ice (i.e., in the preparatory phase) 3-4 training sessions are recommended for the 9 and 10 year olds.

■ In the course of the main period, besides the three training sessions on the ice weekly there should also be 1-2 training sessions off the ice.

■ The training session on the ice should last 60-75 minutes and off the ice about 90 minutes.

■ Each training session should include a game on a short pitch as well as one using the whole pitch.

■ As soon as the players can partially master the recommended skills, attack and defense actions should be practiced equally.

■ When training children, devote individual time to each and in groups, use different forms of groups.

■ Sufficient numbers of assistants should help with the training.

■ Each training session starts with a greeting and ends with a discussion group. The players must be positively motivated.

■ The individual exercises should last 5-7 minutes.

■ Just like in the category of the 6-8 year olds, at this age it is recommended to change the players round the various positions (except as goalie).

■ Always select the optimum form of training in relation to the number of players (see "Hockey – First Steps for Kids").

■ Use various methods of organizing games relative and adequate for the area being used and the number of participants.

■ For preparing the training sessions and for keeping a record of training data, a training diary should be maintained.

■ Pay regard to the completeness of the player's equipment and the correct length of the sticks.

# Tips for Framework Plans

## 5.1 Plan Framework – 9 Year Olds

### Theory
- Ice hockey rules – basic terminology.
- Basic hygiene.
- Daily routine.

### Skating
- Perfecting all of the skills already mastered.
- Tight circles and braking.
- Maneuvering.
- Changing direction – forwards, backwards, sideways.

### Dribbling the puck
- Perfecting all the variations already mastered (short and long dribbling, close and open dribbling, push shots and pressing).
- Dribbling the puck without visual control.
- Further variations of dodging maneuvers.

### Breaking out free with the puck
- Perfecting the basic variation of the feinting maneuver (with the puck, body (aka body deke), stick).
- Getting to be able to do the short and long feinting maneuvers automatically.
- Further variations of the feinting maneuver.
- Practicing the 1:1 attack situation.

### Breaking out free without the puck
- By changing direction and speed.
- Basic action for building up an attack in the defense zone and the neutral zone – skate forwards in a sideways position with a forwards curve.

### Passing and receiving the puck
- Perfecting the skills for passing and receiving a pass (on the forehand, backhand) over short and long distances.
- Practicing long passes.
- Passing over a hurdle.
- Angle passes.
- Various ways of receiving inaccurate passes.

### Shooting techniques
- Improvement of the wrist shot.
- Doing a slap shot.
- Shooting out of an evading action and after a pass.
- Rebound shots and intentional fake shots (tip-in).
- Completing actions in the immediate vicinity of the goal.

### Marking the opposing player with the puck
- Hooking the puck out with the stick.
- Attacking the opponent by skating forwards in the attack zone – direction and angle of movement, contact with the opponent.
- Covering the opponent who is dribbling the puck by skating backwards – correct positioning, close marking.
- Gaining puck possession in 1:1s.

### Marking the opposing player without the puck
- Marking the opposing player without the puck – correct positioning.

### Covering the ice
- Division of the ice into zones.

### Collective team play
- Situation 2:0 and 2:1.
- "Passing and skating".
- Basic actions when building up the attack from the defense zone.
- Layout of the defense formation 2-1-2, basic formations in all the playing zones.

### Face-off
- Basics (positioning, holding the stick etc.).
- Layout formations of own players – in own half 3:2.
- Two simple face-off techniques – individual actions, playing the puck back.
- All players get to practice the face-off.

### Play
- Play a game on the whole of the ice; play in one of the zones (mini-hockey); various preparatory games (different numbers of players and spatial situation).

## 5.2 Plan Framework – 10 Year Olds

### Theory
- Ice hockey rules – revision and improving knowledge.
- Basic hygiene.
- Daily routine.

### Skating
- Perfecting all of the skills already mastered.
- Doing rapid cross-over skating steps in the curve.
- Ending tight curves and braking.
- Changing direction.

### Dribbling the puck
- Dribbling the puck without visual control.
- Further variations of dodging maneuvers.

### Breaking out free with the puck
- Faking a shot and doing feinting maneuvers in a 1:1 situation under difficult circumstances.
- Kicking the puck away when doing a feinting maneuver.
- Practicing new variations of the feinting maneuver.
- Breaking out free into exposed areas (covering the whole ice).

### Passing and receiving the puck
- Perfecting passing and receiving a pass skills over long distances.
- Using the skate to take control of the puck.
- Practicing high passes.

### Shooting techniques
- Practice and improvement of the slap shot.
- Practice and improvement of a shot into the upper corner of the goal after a pass.
- Shooting into specific corners of the goal.
- Agility in front of the goal when doing a shot.
- Firming up techniques for rebound shots and intentional fake shots (tip-in).

### Marking the opposing player with the puck
- Body techniques against an opponent on the boards and in the corners.
- Practicing body checking.

### Marking the opposing player without the puck
- Close marking the opposing player without the puck.
- Marking the distance between the opponent with the puck and another opponent without the puck.
- Covering and marking the area between the opponent and one's own goal.

### Blocking shots and stopping the puck
- In a standing position and on one knee/both knees.
- Stopping the puck with a sideways gliding swing stop.

## Collective team play

- Passing and skating (aka "Give and go").
- Winning situations 2:1.
- Cooperating with 2:0; 3:0 and 3:1.
- Crossing.
- Leaving a pass for the player behind (aka the "drop pass").
- Basics of taking on the puck, defending and building cover.
- Perfecting the basic actions when building up the attack from the defense zone.
- Layout of the defense formation 2-1-2, basic formations in all the playing zones. Basic layout when the center forward (left wing player) is pulled back. No particular game play is apportioned ('defense to the last man').
- Playing short-handed – layout of the four players in the defense zone.

## Face-off

- Basics – individual actions, backwards.
- Layout formations of own players – 3:2.
- All players get to practice the face-off.

## Play

- Play a game on the whole of the ice.
- Play in one of the zones (mini-hockey).
- Various preparatory games (different numbers of players and spatial situation).

# 6 Building up Attack Training

## 6.1 Breaking out Free with the Puck

The player who breaks out free with the puck intends to create an outnumbering situation for the forwards over the opponents and this type of action is gaining in importance in modern ice hockey. The reason for this is the fact that, at the moment, there is very little difference between the individual teams regarding fitness and tactics. So that a team can create a goal scoring opportunity, it does this by creating an outnumbered situation with its players in the most important part of the ice. Maneuvering and clever passing moves no longer achieve a result, instead at least one defense player has to be played round. The basic techniques of this individual game play (puck dribbling and dodging) were comprehensively covered in my book "Hockey – First Steps for Kids". Before going on to the next complicated technique, it should be emphasized again that breaking out free with the puck must be accompanied by further attacking actions – dodging and feinting. In ice hockey training methods and training, however, these are covered separately. When the player has mastered the basic techniques of these individual skills (puck dribbling, dodging maneuvers and faking shots), then he must work at automating these and practice them regularly.

## 6.2 Dodging and Feinting

The effectiveness of a player breaking out free relies not only on the mastering of the technique, but also on the accompanying actions (fake shots and feinting). The attacker attempts to confuse the opponent, by making a feinting movement (i.e., a normal action is intimated, but not carried out). The opponent believes a particular action will follow but then something else is carried out.

The following different variations of dodging and feinting are possible:
- With the body.
- By changing direction and speed.
- By moving the stick.

In practice, all these variations are carried out either separately or as a combination of one or the other.

## Feinting with the body

Feinting with the body is done by making a head, shoulder, and arm or hip movement. The main aim is to get the defending player to make a movement in the wrong direction.

The puck is being dribbled on the forehand side of the player and the stick is being held in both hands. The player with the puck bends forward to the left (or right) in a short movement just before he reaches the defender. He then begins to lead the puck in that direction. By doing this he is giving the impression of trying to outplay the defender down that side. The movement is made with a short sideways twist of the head, shoulders and upper body combined with a shift of balance onto the gliding leg. As soon as the opponent reacts, the attacker pushes off from the gliding leg into the other direction with an increase in speed. The attacker plays the puck under the defender's stick and brings it onto the other side (see Diagram 1). In this variation, it is important to keep the eye on the defender and carry out the feinting movement so that he is forced to react too soon. Feinting can also be done by moving the legs. This kind of movement demands a perfect ice-skating technique and generally this is only achievable by older players. The practical effectiveness of this variation is very high.

A further possible variation is the combination of several feinting movements of the body and the shoulders sideways with an increase in speed as the player takes off in the other direction, with the result that the defender cannot follow.

**Diagram 1**

## Feinting by changing direction

Feinting by changing direction demands good ice-skating techniques. This variation can be carried out in two different ways. The first method is doing cross-over steps and the second one is to skate in fast, tight circles. As mentioned already, this skill depends on being able to break out free with the puck by changing direction and speed. By changing direction using the cross-over step (weaving) the attacker does cross-over steps rapidly in both directions, well before he gets near the defender. Important here is high speed and sufficient room. At the moment the opponent reacts, the attacker rapidly changes direction into a clear space. Similarly, one can use playing a tap-through or outplaying the opponent etc.

The second possibility, which uses skating fast, tight circles, is more suitable where the opponent is behind the attacker. The attacker is standing on both skates and by unweighting the pressure on them, he turns both skates in one direction, digging the edges into the ice as he does. This whole movement is then generally done again to the other side. The difficult part of the maneuver is rapidly unweighting the pressure on the skates and turning with sufficient thrust onto their edges at the same time. As the opponent reacts, the attacker moves off to the clear side. It is important to dribble the puck away from the body and protect it with the inclined blade of the stick.

## Feinting by changing speed

The player skates along constantly changing speed and rhythm. This makes things difficult for the defender. We can imagine a situation where the attacker with the puck abruptly brakes from high speed in front of the defender and then skates off rapidly again.

The next possibility is for the attacker to skate along slowly trying to get the opponent to match his speed. At the right moment, the attacker rapidly increases speed and frees himself from the defender. Other feinting movements (with the body and with the stick) can also be combined with this so that the player can break out free with the puck.

## Dodging and feinting by moving the stick

Dodging and feinting with the stick can be divided into several variations. The basic three variations, however, are:

- Feinting by moving the stick without touching the puck.
- Feinting by faking a pass.
- Feinting by faking a shot.

## Feinting by moving the stick without touching the puck

The player leads the puck with the blade of the stick held protecting it closely. Moving rapidly to one side he indicates his direction. He brings the blade over the puck again as if to move it across to the other side (opposite to where he indicated). As usual, feinting movements with the body and the shoulders are also used.

## Feinting by faking a pass

A faked pass is very effective when dribbling, because the defenders usually react with a movement. A faked pass gives the passer and his teammates time to decide what to do next.

The player with the puck fakes (moving the stick, turning the shoulders and head) a pass to a teammate. By exaggerating the rotation of the stick blade head, the direction of the pass is intimated (at the same time a glance is thrown in that direction). After starting the movement of the stick head, the blade head is laid tightly over the other side and the player breaks out free from the opponent.

## Feinting by faking a shot

The attacker brings his stick back up high. As soon as the defender makes a defensive move (pulling the legs together, bringing the body upright, throwing himself at the shot), he has committed himself and cannot do any other action (push-off start etc.). The attacker gathers the puck up quickly and carries out a sideways dodging maneuver and increases speed.

## Further variations of breaking out free with the puck

Perfect puck dribbling while skating forwards and backwards (all technical variations) and the skill of breaking out free with the puck (all variations) are absolutely necessary for training the skills covered here. As already mentioned, dodging and feinting are of course also the main ingredients of the method of breaking out free with the puck. To make the feinting movement effective, the player has to judge the correct moment to apply it. Because of this he has to have a good feeling for 'space' (judging distances). Feinting movements and dodging are the most difficult technical elements. They demand a correct and quick reaction by the player and require good movement coordination ability. The trainer of this age group must realize that, at the beginning of training, the players will hardly be able to master these techniques. Despite this, it is recommended to include them in the training, step by step, thus establishing a basis for improvement when they get older. In later stages of training, these skills will be developed further with the aim of achieving stability and variability in movement sequences even under difficult conditions. These include, in particular, unusual psychological conditions (nervousness and fear), tiredness, the active resistance of the opponent and limitations in time and space.

In mastering the skill of breaking out free, the player dribbling the puck has to rely on certain principles. Amongst these, the most important ones are:

- Constant contact with the puck using the blade head of the stick.
- Good peripheral vision.
- Handling the stick quickly when controlling the puck.
- Dodging and feinting – with the head, body, by moving the stick, changing direction and speed rapidly.
- Covering the puck using the body.
- Keeping an eye on the defending player and his stick.
- Increasing speed after the dodging and feinting movement.

The technical execution of breaking out free skills by the player with the puck influences tactics, which have to be gone into, discussed and practiced. With appropriate regard for the mental and technical development of the young players, the trainer introduces the individual game situations and explains to them that techniques and tactics when breaking out free with the puck are dependent on the following factors:

- Game situation.
- The area on the ice where the skills are put into action.
- Defensive actions by the opponent.
- Quality and quantity of the skills mastered.
- The correct selection of the technique and the speed of reaction.
- Experience.

There are yet further variations of the skill of breaking out free with the puck that also use dodging and feinting. In no way will this be an exhaustive list. It is, however, important that the young players get to learn as many techniques as possible, so that they can at least make use of some, which they feel comfortable with according to their own individual skills and ability. When older, the best players can make use of dodging and feinting skills devised by themselves. They must be able to use them to perfection in any game situation.

## Methodical tips

Training for dodging and feinting is begun, first of all, after the basics of learning to dribble with the puck and to make evading maneuvers. Later on, they should become a firm part of every evading movement:

- Training is done, first of all, standing still to both sides (backhand and forehand).
- Separate training is conducted for the individual feinting movements.
- Practicing skating slowly with aids (cones, stands etc.).
- At the beginning, the players may watch the puck as they control it, but later on they have to use peripheral vision only, and by just getting a feeling for play (various exercises – the trainer indicates the number of repeats to be done by the players by putting up his fingers etc.).
- Training is conducted at slow speed with one player acting as a free defender.
- Afterwards, the exercises are conducted at full speed.
- The trainer emphasizes the automation of the relationship between the sequences feinting – evading – increasing speed with a kick-off.
- Combining various evading and feinting movements.
- Exercises for achieving the high coordination demands of the cycle feinting – evading – increasing speed with a kick-off.
- Using the feinting and evading variations in a game situation 1:1.

## Main mistakes

- Constant control of the puck with the eyes (the attacker does not watch the opponent and his stick).
- The feinting movement is not carried out prior to the evading movement.
- The evading movement is carried out too early or on the contrary too far away from the opponent.
- The feinting movement is not successful – the opponent does not react.
- After carrying out the feinting movement, the player does not skate past the opponent nor does he increase his speed.
- The player uses an unsuitable feinting movement or uses the same one, over and over again, to the same side.

## Protecting the puck using the body in free areas

By using this form of protecting technique, the player learns how to keep the puck out of the range of the defender. The player has to be in the right position between the puck and the defender. This variation of dribbling is the same as done in skating curves (short curves, cross-over steps).

When the opponent attacks a player from the side or from behind and the player with the puck changes direction (he skates into a curve), he switches his center of gravity onto his bent inside leg. The other leg is being held out wider, more to the rear, and at the same time his back is turned towards the opponent. To protect the puck from hooking out attempts or stick knocks/lifts, the inside shoulder and inside leg, which is bent into the curve, are both pushed forward a little. The puck is being lead with the stick arm outstretched diagonally slightly to the rear and as far away from the body as possible. The other arm is there to ward off the opponent or his stick. The blade of the stick must be angled towards the puck. Similar to covering the puck by skating circles, cross-over steps can be practiced. There are two variations – on the forehand side and on the backhand side.

For left-handed players, when moving to the left, the left hand carries out the warding off function (to hold the opponent's stick down) (see Diagram 2).

**Diagram 2**

### Main mistakes

- When skating into a tight curve, the player is holding himself too upright (knees are not bent sufficiently).
- The head of the blade of the stick is not inclined enough over the puck.
- The player is not between the puck and an opponent.
- The puck is being dribbled too near to the body.

## Protecting the puck on the boards

In game situations on the boards, it is important that a player can protect the puck well when he is faced frontally onto the boards. The young player has to be taught that the main aim is not to hold the puck up against the boards, but to get out of this unfavorable position as quickly as possible. In other words – the training is not only about executing a successful technique of protecting the puck on the boards, but also about skating off freely with the puck away from the boards.

The player with the puck is facing frontally onto the boards and is between the opponent and the puck. The player has managed to lever himself away from the boards sufficiently, thus avoiding being pinned against them. A broad split leg position will give him sufficient stability. He is able, at the same time, to protect the puck by using his legs bent well at the knee. The tips of the skates are pointing inwards (exactly like in the full plough). The stick is being held, according to the situation, in one or both hands. The free arm can ward off the opponent or be used to push the player with the puck off the boards. It is important to hold the stick correctly – the stick should not be in a right-angled position between the player and the boards. The knob end of the shaft of the stick must be turned away from the body, otherwise it could cause injuries, and also, if the knob end is blocked, the player with the puck will have no opportunity to play it, or even pass it on (see Diagram 3).

**Diagram 3**

**Main mistakes**

- The player with the puck is too close to the boards.
- Poor stability and balance (the center of gravity of the body is not sunk down enough; the split legged position is not broad enough; the tips of the skates are not turned in enough) – the defender can easily pin the player with the puck hard against the boards and block him there so that he cannot pass the puck out.
- The stick of the player with the puck is blocked.

## Breaking out free by using a turn

The attacking player with the puck executes a quick turn after doing a rapid braking movement, either one-sided or swinging stop with both legs. The turn can be to either side – the forehand or the backhand. The player with the puck (the left-hander) is coming from the right and feints a shot or a pass on the unfavorable side. The defender wants to prevent this and goes to that side. At that moment, the attacker brakes rapidly with a swinging stop (the skates are almost parallel) and plays the puck through his own legs and then executes a turn on the rear leg.

A similar variation is one-sided braking (in Russian publications called the "Spirale"). The attacker brakes on one leg near to the opponent, turns his back round and dribbles the puck off onto the side of his rear leg and executes a turn (see Diagram 4).

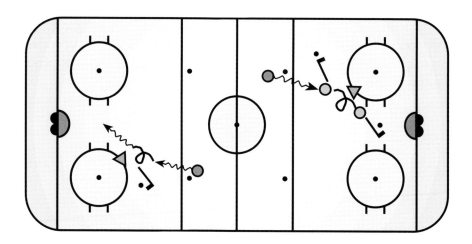

**Diagram 4**

A further variation is the rapid half-turn. At the moment that the player with the puck turns his back on the opponent and feints that he is continuing the turn, he changes the direction of the turn and ends it in the originally planned direction.

## Breaking out free by changing direction and speed – stopping – starting

This variation is also a feinting movement. Its execution depends on good puck dribbling techniques and protecting the puck when stopping and starting. Quick stopping power (one-sided or a swinging stop) with a rapid start (involving the possibility of changing direction) away from the opponent.

This variation should be explained and demonstrated to the beginner for execution on both sides. In the first method, the attacking player stops quickly and then pushes off starting in the same direction. In the second method, he starts off to one side after stopping, taking the puck with him in that direction (see Diagram 5).

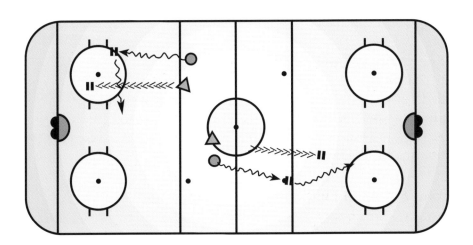

**Diagram 5**

The player brakes either one-sided or with a swinging stop, each time stopping between the opponent and the puck, which is kept as far away from the body as possible (puck being protected). Preparatory exercises for this skill are exercises like copy cat, changing direction on a signal and following a partner (see Exercises in Chapter 16).

## Breaking out free by moving the puck with the skate (stick – ice-skate – stick)

This variation can be also practiced in at least two different methods. In the first method, at the moment that the player is immediately in front of the opponent (his stick), the player with the puck pulls the puck back onto his ice-skate, which is held at right angles to the puck. The puck is pushed forward into a clear area by the ice-skate and is picked up by the stick. In the second, relatively complicated method, the attacker is standing on both legs in a sideways split legged stance with one leg slightly forward. The hockey stick and the puck are out to the left, away from the body, on the forehand side (for a left-handed player). When the opponent attacks, the player pulls the puck quickly diagonally back on to the right ice-skate, which is slightly set back to the rear and turned. Without loss of speed, he kicks the puck forward with his right foot onto the stick, which is in front. In both methods, it is important, to carry out the maneuver as near to the opponent as possible and then to protect the puck with the leg, body or hand (to prevent the opposition intervening).

## Faked loss of the puck

About 1-2m away from the defender, the attacker (right-handed) leaves the puck on the side (the forehand side is better) and fakes that he has lost it by skating a little to the left. As the defender starts towards the puck, the attacker pulls the puck quickly forwards and switches it over to the other side and accelerates. The puck must be brought in as close as possible to the ice-skates so that the defender cannot carry out an attack.

## Feinting movement with a change of direction

This feinting movement for a player with the puck consists of feinting a movement in one direction, breaking out free in another direction, stopping half way through and then switching back to skating in the original direction. The attacker places the center of gravity of his body to the right (left) taking the puck with him. There is then a movement back to the left (right). The defender reacts, convinced that the attacker is trying to outplay him to the left (right). The player with the puck, however, abruptly changes direction and breaks out free to the right (left).

## Feinting movement down the middle

The attacker fakes a feinting movement by using his shoulders and upper body that he is coming down the centerline of attack. At the last second, just in front of the defender, the player brings his stick with the puck in the direction of the boards. At this moment it is important that the player's body is between the opponent and the puck. The stick is held in an outstretched hand. With his free arm and his backside, he provides protection for the puck at an adequate distance from the opponent (see Diagram 6).

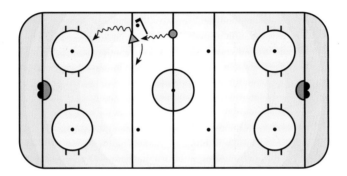

**Diagram 6**

## Feinting movement with a fake towards the boards

The player with the puck fakes that he is going to mount an attack along the sides by the boards. The defender maintains close contact with him in order to try to pin him against the boards. At that moment, the attacking player brakes slightly and plays off the boards round the opponent. The attacker outplays him round and down the other side (see Diagram 7).

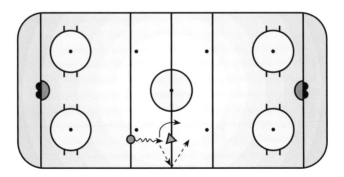

**Diagram 7**

## Braking and doing a push-off start again

The attacking player skates along – for example along the sides by the boards. The defending player tries to get up close to him. Because of this the attacker stops abruptly (one-sided or with a swinging stop) facing the boards frontally. As soon as the defender also stops, the player pushes-off with a quick start in the originally planned direction (see Diagram 8).

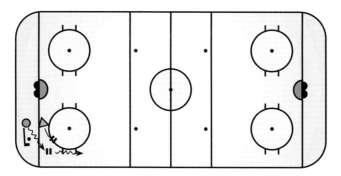

**Diagram 8**

## Changing direction

The attacker dribbles the puck at the end of the ice and at times behind the goal. Just prior to the defender coming into contact, he executes a swinging curved stop with his legs well bent and starts off in the opposite direction (see Diagram 9).

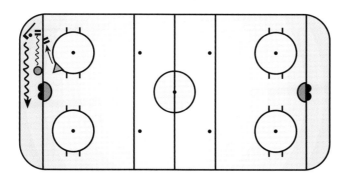

**Diagram 9**

## Evasive action in the opposite direction

This variation of breaking out free is often used in a game after entering the attack zone behind the blue line. The player with the puck moves along the boards quickly (preferably with the puck on the side where the boards are). Protection of the puck using the body and protection against the opponent's stick gives the impression that he wants to skate deep into the playing zone. At that moment, as the defender attacks him, the player with the puck executes a rapid, tight, braked curve (with the knees well bent) into a whole twist turn followed up by a rapid skate off into the middle of the playing zone, or alternatively he passes the puck to an unmarked teammate. When skating into the curve and turn, control of the puck and its protection by a properly inclined blade head are important (see Diagram 10).

**Diagram 10**

## Methodical tips

- From all the breaking out variations that are included here, only those techniques should be selected that the young players can achieve at any one time.
- Each technique should be perfectly demonstrated (best of all by a player from the 1st Team or using a video recording). A complete explanation of the movements is also essential.
- The exercises are done first of all standing still and then at a slow pace.
- After the technique can be mastered when standing still, the movements are practiced slowly by using cones, stands etc.
- At the beginning, the players may watch the puck as they control it, but later on they have to use peripheral vision only, and by just getting a feeling for play (various exercises – the trainer indicates the number of repeats to be done by the players by putting up his fingers etc.).
- The feinting movements are done first of all against a passive, defending player (without stick or with his stick reversed etc.).
- Practice special exercises for individual breaking out free variations by the dribbling player.
- Training for combination of feinting movements with further game play (feinting, shooting, passing).
- Game play exercises in the various game zones 1:1.

## The main mistakes in the technique

- Constant control of the puck with the eyes (the attacker does not watch the opponent).
- Individual feinting actions taking too long to execute – the defender has time to react to the attacker's actions.
- The breaking out free variations are only carried out down one side.
- The player concentrates too much on the feinting movement and forgets to increase his speed or shoot.
- The player executes the game play actions without moving quickly forwards (he is always standing on both legs).

## Game situations 1:1 (Attack)

In a situation one-to-one, with direct passes to the attacker, individual actions are part of the main features of team play. Taking on an opponent requires good puck control by the attacker with the puck, and where this is the case, the teammate without the puck can take part in the action without having to worry about the other losing the puck.

Every 1:1 game situation has a specific solution. It is, therefore, important that the trainer concentrates not only on the loading in training, but that he also explains the activity (technique and tactics) and demonstrates all the possible solutions. As soon as the young players are able to master the basics (required for breaking out free with the puck), they should also be able to master particular 1:1 situations from a technical and tactical point of view. First of all, they have to decide whether they are going to dribble the puck and try to win a 1:1 situation or simply pass the puck on or shoot at goal. In all the exercises, the players should not be watching the puck but keeping an eye on the opponent. At the same time, of course, they should keep watch where their own teammates are on the ice.

From this it is clear that a good player not only has to possess technical knowledge, he also has to be well-versed in tactical knowledge and skills. A technical skill is only effective when it is used correctly in a game. The trainer has to select those exercises, which resemble as closely as possible game situations and game conditions. Solutions for 1:1 game situations (in competition and in training) are influenced by three basic factors:

- The area where the situation occurs – game zone (defense, neutral and attack zone), the angle of play, the corners, the blue attack and defense lines, the boards, shooting area, area behind the goal.
- The individual technical and tactical ability of the defender – his good points and his weaknesses, ice-skating variations and direction (backwards or forwards), whether he attacks from the side or skates up from behind, ice-skating skills and strength etc.
- The individual technical and tactical ability of the attacker.

## Puck control in a confined area

Before going on to give the characteristics of solutions for 1:1 situations in the individual game zones, the subject of puck control in a confined area will be covered. There are situations where play occurs in the corners, along the boards, behind the goal line, in the goal area, in the middle of the ice (where there are lots of players skating) and in the areas along the blue lines (see Diagram 11).

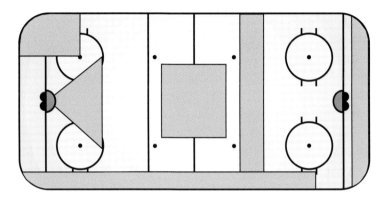

**Diagram 11**

Action in a confined space, under pressure (situation 1:1) demands a high degree of coordination and specific playing agility. Rapid changes of direction and speed, turns, stops and starts have to be accomplished. Besides this the puck has to be protected by the body and the arm (covering) and also the opponent's stick has to be blocked.

Step by step, the young players are taught the technical and tactical solutions in a 1:1 situation. First of all this is done individually and later done as teamwork. In training practice, the mistake is often made of training these kinds of situations in the center of the playing area without any pressure on the player with the puck. This mistake has a negative effect on progress of the player's performance. The player must get to experience these situations in all the playing areas, above all in the attack zone, ending up with a shot at goal (from a suitable shooting angle). The youngsters should learn the various solutions in such a way, so that they are in a position when older to be able to act, using an optimum solution in combination with their own improvisation and creativity.

Besides the actual individual solution, the cooperation of players without the puck is an important factor when playing in a confined space. In particular, this means using supporting passing movements, rapid transition of play into a free area and combinations, based on players swapping round their positions on the ice.

## Solutions for the 1:1 situation – dependent on space available

As already mentioned, the playing area, in which 1:1 actions happen, is the main, important factor governing the selection of a solution. With a few exceptions, we are talking about limited (confined) spaces:

- Round the central axis of the playing area.
- Along the boards.
- Behind the goal line.
- In the corners.
- On the blue attack and defense lines.
- In the individual playing zones (defense, neutral and attack zones).
- The shooting area in front of the goal in the attack zone.

### a]   1:1 situation round the central axis of the playing area

The central axis of the playing area (particularly in the neutral zone) gives the attacker, on the one hand, plenty of space to move in and plenty of opportunity to use dodging and feinting movements. On the other hand, this area is sometimes defined as a 'confined' space because of the number of players present in it at any one time. The attacker can use a short evading movement combined with a feint as well as carrying out a longer evading movement and outplay his opponent at high speed. Breaking out free using a turn, playing round, changing direction and speed combined with a simultaneously executed feint with the body and stick are also just as effective. Breaking out free with the puck is necessary in a 1:1 situation when:

- The player is not the last player in front of his own goal.

- The player is not in such a position where the loss of the puck could endanger his own goal.

- The player cannot see a teammate in front of him in a better position (when looking at the opposing goal).

In connection with this, play in the neutral zone should also be referred to. In comparison with the other playing zones, it is wrong to consider the neutral zone as unimportant. Of course, it is very rare to score goals from here (except following a mistake by the goalie).

The importance of the neutral zone lies, nevertheless, mainly in the possible use of various technical and tactical variations, which can be executed in a relatively clear space not far away from the opposing goal. The young players must be made to realize that the aim of an attack is not only to bridge the neutral zone, but that it is in this space that the attack is developed further and speeded up. If these demands are fulfilled, not only game actions but also a pass into the path of a free teammate will be possible. Before closing with a defender, the attacker should bring his movements down to match those of the defender.

When the attacking player has a clear space, it is a good move to do cross-over steps in both directions with simultaneous feinting movements of the body and stick, just as the defender is approached. These actions force the defender to make a sideways movement and makes defending difficult. This moment is good for a feinting movement, catching the defender off-balance as he goes the wrong way – a simple, practice exercise for this is depicted in Diagram 12.

Another variation is rapid, aggressive skating towards the defender, who has to make an evading action. This gives the attacker greater space to maneuver in or pass the puck.

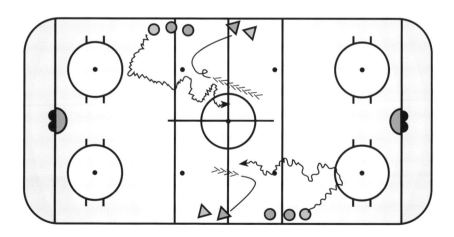

**Diagram 12**

When attacked by an opponent, if the player with the puck carries out a long maneuver mainly in the neutral zone, he creates free space from which both of them can skate through. In the free space a teammate may well be in a good position to accept a pass. At the same time, this action makes the opponent's defense very difficult. A long, drawn out maneuver, with rapid changes of direction and speed by the player with the puck close up to the defender, makes it extremely difficult for the opponents to follow the puck (see Diagram 13).

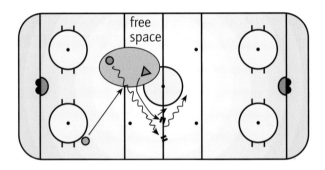

free
space

**Diagram 13**

### b]   1:1 situation in the shooting zone

The area, near the goal in the attacking zone (the so-called shooting area) is where shots at goal can be made against the defending players covering that goal. This is sometimes more effective than doing a feinting movement. In this situation, it is important to deliver a hard, accurate shot that also surprises. The attacker shoots when:

- ....he is in the shooting area near the goal (favorable tactical situation).
- ....the defender is standing in a firm defensive position in front of the goal or when the player moves quickly into the shooting area.
- ....the defending player blocks the goalie's field of vision.
- ....the area in front of the goal is full of players.
- ....he is attacked by the opponent.
- ....the goalie is not in an optimum, defensive position (in goal).
- ....no other teammate is in a better position to shoot at goal.

The attacker has two possibilities when delivering the shot past the defender. One possibility, which requires a certain amount of time and space, is to do a feinting, evading movement on the backhand with a simultaneous, quick switchover of the

stick to the forehand, followed up by a quick wrist shot. It is important that, when the attacker pulls his stick back for the shot, he frees himself from the defender, who otherwise could block the shot.

The second possibility is for the attacker to deliver a surprise shot past the defender just as he does a feinting movement. In training, the shot past the defender should be practiced from various situations e.g., directly from central axis of the playing area; or doing a rush-in to the shooting area from the boards; from the corner or from the area behind the goal. After doing the first possibility, the older players can then practice the second possibility in the same 1:1 situation skating on the other side (see Diagram 14).

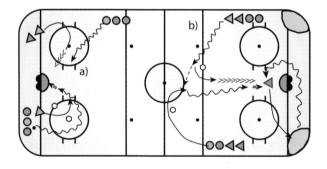

**Diagram 14**

### c] 1:1 situation on the boards

The area along the boards considerably limits the number of moves that an attacking player can make. At the same time it makes the defender's job easier. Therefore, the attacker faces greater tactical demands. Shooting at goal in such cases is of course more complicated. Exercises in 1:1 situations are just as suitable for practicing from along the boards as well as from areas behind the goal in both the playing end zones. In these exercises, the opponent not only has to skate backwards to defend, he can also attack the player with the puck from his side or skate up behind him and attack him from there. The next diagram 'a)' shows a tackling action along the boards in a confined space (between the boards and the cones) with the defender skating backwards. In the 'b)' variation of the exercise, the player with the puck is attacked from the side. Young players should also practice breaking out free with a feint. In the second version, where the player is attacked from the side, good puck control and a break out free possibility using a change in direction (rapid curves, stopping) or speed (stopping – starting again) are both particularly important. Later on, further variations of breaking out free are described e.g., chasing after the opponent (backchecking) etc.

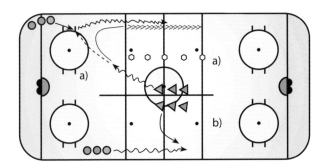

**Diagram 15**

After learning the basic techniques, exercises are done where the players break out free after coming up against close defense. In a game, such cases are mainly the actions of breaking out free from the defender in one's own tight defensive zone, or from the tight area in the attacking zone as well as from frontal positions and rear positions when attacking the opponent. An important requirement for additional ways of breaking out free is the efficient control of the puck along the boards (skating front on to them). To break out free, the best form is to do an evading movement with a feint while in the middle of the playing area followed by a short pause and then an evading movement with a feint towards the boards – starting in the center of the playing area, turning, playing round the opposition and accelerating rapidly.

Specific situations crop up in a game where the puck is behind the goal and it requires getting it into the shooting area. Solutions for this make high technical and tactical demands on the player. The situation for the goalie is more dangerous where the attacking player frees it round to the forehand side. When the player with the puck skates in behind the goal, he should use the goal itself to give the puck protection. This means leading the puck along quite close to the goal and where the defender may not get in between the puck and the goal. When the player is able to skate fast enough and have sufficient space, he skates quickly out from behind the goal and either shoots or passes the puck out to a teammate standing in a better position. Another version is to change direction and skate back again along the original path. In such a case, the player will do several feinting movements before he skates out into a free area in front of the goal (see Diagram 16).

**Diagram 16**

### d]    1:1 situation in the corner

The corners of the rink are not very suitable to carry out solutions for 1:1 situations. This is because in the tight, restricted area (and thus no great possibility to carry out maneuvers) it just seems to get tighter. Breaking out free from here demands good ice-skating techniques (quick changes of direction, starts and stops) and simultaneously excellent puck control. The puck is brought into the area just in front of the opponent's goal. Of course, this is exactly where the opponent is going to defend the hardest.

Training for these situations is often underestimated in practice sessions. The special exercises for it are seldom used. However, because these technically demanding situations often occur, the young players must have already practiced them. In the corner, the player can free himself and make the opponent confused mainly by employing changes of direction – turns, stopping and starting again – and by changes of direction coupled with a feinting movement (dodging and faking). The exercise consists of the player with the puck turning his back on the opponent and facing the playing area (see Diagram 17). The next diagram shows an exercise example with main emphasis on the player with the puck breaking out free from the corner and then skating into the shooting zone. When this exercise has been done, the same exercise is done from the other corner with a change of roles of the defender and the attacker.

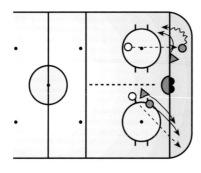

**Diagram 17**

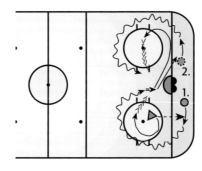

**Diagram 18**

Besides individual game situations, there are those that occur in the corner that are resolved between players with and without the puck. Short, supporting passes between 2-3 players as well as assistance by a player shielding or screening the opponent to prevent him intervening. Such solutions, however, are more suitable for older players and therefore will be described later.

### e] 1:1 situation penetrating the attacking zone

Crossing the blue line into the attacking zone is done either by coming through the center of the rink or down along the boards. As mentioned already, these are confined spaces where the solution demands that the attacker has a high degree of technical and tactical prowess. The situation over the blue line down the central axis into the attacking zone already means that the defender will try to threaten the action. On the other hand, if the puck is lost as the attacking zone is entered, there will be a danger of a counter-attack.

Young players must learn several variations of penetrating the attacking zone (each time with the emphasis on completing the whole action). Exercises, where the action ends up in the corner of the attacking zone, are not recommended at all. When crossing into the attacking zone down the central part of the rink, the player uses the normal variations to outplay the opponent (with use also of the action of shooting past him). As mentioned already, the area down the central axis of the rink is better than the area down the boards for breaking out free and building up the attack.

In the event that the attacker finds himself moving along the boards in the attacking zone, besides the normal evading feinting maneuvers and outplaying the opponent there are also other possibilities of getting past.

The next diagram shows a situation where the defender is having to skate backwards up as far as the face-off circle. As he conducts a 'rush' movement across the blue line, the player with the puck forces the defender to create a large gap. The attacker then slows down and this achieves sufficient space between him and the opponent without coming into contact with him (one speaks often of a so-called 'delaying tactic'). Space, achieved in this way, is then used by the attacker to do a tight circling movement back into the center of the rink. He then increases his skating speed so that he can get into the shooting zone along the central axis. The action is ended by either making a shot at goal or by skating parallel to the blue line and passing the puck to a teammate, who is in a better position to shoot.

**Diagram 19**

There is another situation where the attacker is in contact with the defending player. For this there are only two exercise variations. In the first case, the attacker feints a movement to play round the opponent (along the boards). Good puck control and cover, using the body, as well as preparedness to ward off the opponent's stick give the impression that the player is looking to penetrate deep into the attacking zone. At a suitable moment, the attacker does a tight, braking curve with well-bent knees, does a turn and skates into the shooting area. Here, delivering a shot at goal (see Diagram 20) completes the action. This exercise can be practiced later together with a teammate without the puck.

**Diagram 20**

In the second case, the attacker plays round the opponent down along the boards and tries to reach the shooting zone (practice on the forehand and on the backhand) before the defender. It is important to cover the puck with the body correctly. If the puck is being dribbled with the stick in one hand, the other arm and hand can be used to ward off the opponent or his stick.

**f]    1:1 situation – How good is the opponent?**
In coming up with solutions for 1:1 situations, it is important to be able to judge the opponent correctly (his strengths and weaknesses). Feinting movements should be done down the defending opponent's strong side so that playing round him happens

down the other side – his weak side. Feinting movements done against a large, not very mobile defender can be done in various directions. In this way he will be forced to move in one direction while the attacker chooses to go down the other side. On the other hand, when you come up against a slow player, feinting movements consisting of change of speed are effective.

When you are against a fast, mobile defender, the delaying tactic will be the successful one. If he prefers to tackle hard, then it is recommended that a change of speed tactic away from the boards is used. In cases where the defender skates backwards and does not try to get possession of the puck, then it is always possible to try a shot past him at goal from a suitable distance, or to pass the puck to a teammate in a better shooting position.

The player must always try to select the right moment to do a feinting movement. Learning to develop a feeling for space (judging distance) will benefit any feinting movement. In a clash during tackling, the player with the puck should always attack the opponent first. The attacker must be able to outplay the opponent not only round his 'strong' side but also round his other side – the 'weak' side. Therefore, all the exercises should be practiced from the forehand as well as the backhand side. For this, defenders and attackers can swap over roles for the exercises.

## Methodology

Where the defender skates backwards or when he is skating forwards and attacks the opponent from the side or from behind, from a methodical point of view, the exercises should be kept separate.

In a 1:1 situation, where the defending player is skating backwards in a basic posture, the young player should be taught the so-called **'triangular position'**. This consists of imaginary lines between the position of the skates and the blade of the defender's hockey stick (see Diagram 21).

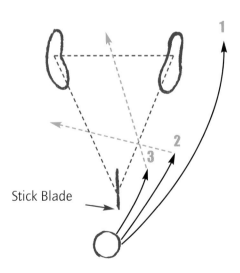

Stick Blade

**Diagram 21**

### Notes to the diagram

**1.** Using skating speed to outplay the opponent and keep control of the puck.

**2.** Feint to the right – skate off to the left, fake right and switch the weight of the body in that direction, play the puck between the stick blade and the opponent's skates.

**3.** Feint to the left, play the puck through between the opponent's skates, skate round the opponent and bring the puck back under control.

The diagram illustrates three basic variations of outplaying the triangle made up of the defender's skates and stick blade. In practice, there are a number of further feinting and dodging maneuvers, like e.g., the fake shot; feint to the right – feint to the left – skate off right, fake losing the puck between the skates etc. They are used as referred to in the notes above. The following tips should be noted:

### Methodical tips

- The defending player (in a position standing still) is in the triangular posture. The player with the puck skates up slowly and uses variation number 1 (skating speed is used to outplay the opponent and keep control of the puck).
- Same situation as in the previous case; the attacker, however, increases his speed following every successful attack on the "triangle".
- The defending player skates slowly backwards.
- The defending player skates backwards gradually increasing his speed. He remains in the basic posture.
- The same as above, but to the other side.
- The same sequence as variation number 2 – "feint to the right – skate off to the left".
- Do variation number 2 in reverse – "feint to the left – skate off to the right".
- Variation No. 3 – skating to the right is done in four stages.
- Variation No. 4 – skating to the left is done in four stages.
- The attacker selects a feinting movement and the defending player adopts the triangular posture; practice this with various different feinting movements.
- The attacker selects a feinting movement and the defending player skates slowly backwards, adopting the triangular posture; practice this with various different feinting movements.
- Same sequence as above, but with an increase in skating speed.
- In the next phase, the defending player shows some opposition, which he intensifies, bit by bit.
- At the end a complete 1:1 situation is practiced.

In order to reach a high degree of efficiency, these actions should be practiced using different variations and repeated often. The exercise can, for example, begin with the attacker on either the boards, in the corner or behind the goal, in the attacking zone or with a full 'rush' down the whole length of the rink. Besides this, the exercises can be constructed to reflect other game situations in certain parts of the rink.

When training, first of all simple exercises with a passive opposition should be carried out. The use of stands or cones can replace the use of another player. As solutions for each situation are mastered, the opposition can be stiffened.

The next diagram shows an example of puck control in a 1:1 situation (without contact). The exercise is carried out in pairs – one player has a stick and the puck and the other one has only a stick. On a signal, the player with the puck plays round his opponent (this variation has already been covered) – play through, play round, feint, change direction etc. As soon as he has outplayed the opponent, he returns and practices it again. On a further signal, the roles are changed over (after about 20-30 seconds). The exercises are made more exacting by:
- introducing physical contact with the defender.
- more use of the stick by the opponent without the puck.

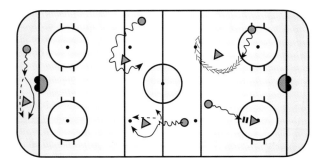

**Diagram 22**

The next diagram shows an exercise with emphasis on covering the puck with the body in a free area. These exercises are done in pairs – the player without a stick and the puck uses only his arms. The player with the puck (with his back towards the opponent) uses his body to cover and protect the puck. He turns his head constantly backwards and forwards (head deke) to keep control of the puck. The exercise is done in a confined space. On a signal, roles are changed over.

*Variations:*

- The defending player uses his stick.
- The exercise is done by three players.

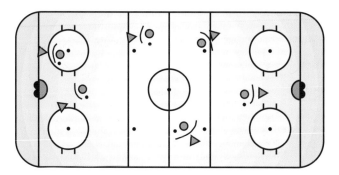

**Diagram 23**

The next diagram illustrates an exercise 1:1 with the puck being covered close to the boards. The player (with his back facing the main playing area) checks the puck using only his ice-skate – he has no stick. He uses only the boards and the Plexiglas screen. The main emphasis is the control of the puck.

*Variations:*

- Both players use sticks.
- The player tries to control two pucks.

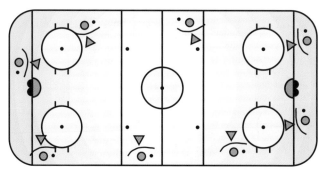

**Diagram 24**

The following diagram shows a basic exercise with the aim of practicing control of the puck under pressure. The players are divided into four groups and play two groups against two groups when a signal is given. The player with the puck tries to get into the shooting area. On a signal the defending group put pressure onto the others.

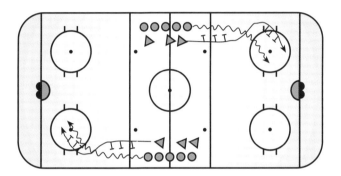

**Diagram 25**

The next diagram illustrates puck control under pressure when the defenders react late. The defending player skates backwards towards the puck and then turns into a forward skating movement. Now the attacker has to cover the puck and control it correctly and get into the shooting area in order to deliver a shot at goal.

*Variations:*

■ The defending player starts off from various postures (kneeling, sitting, and lying down).

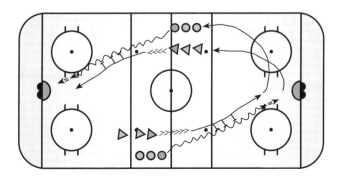

**Diagram 26**

The following diagram illustrates a solution in a 1:1 situation in the attacking zone against a defender skating backwards along the central axis. The defender skates forward round the cone and turns into a backwards skating mode, staying always facing the puck and the opposition. The player with the puck also skates round the cone and tries to outplay the defender using a feinting movement, a fake and a shot at goal past him etc. The defending player has to keep on the move (skating backwards) and remain in contact with the player with the puck. When the players are able to master the situation, a second action can be performed – from the boards (from the corner – section 'a' in the diagram; from the boards – section 'b' in the diagram, or the trainer plays the puck in). The trainer makes sure that positions are changed over regularly.

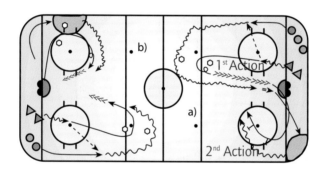

**Diagram 27**

When skating down into the defensive zone, the attacking player finds himself often having to come up with a 1:1 situation solution in the area of the blue defending line. In such a case, the defending player forechecks deep into the zone along the boards (so-called pinching).

The attacker can meet this situation with three basic variations:
- By making a feint with a fake towards the boards and then play round the opponent.
- By making a feint with a fake towards the boards and then breaking out free into the center of the rink.
- By making a feint with a fake towards the center of the rink and then breaking out free along the boards.

In this, the forechecking player plays a training role only (first of all he defends passively − without a stick or with stick reversed etc., so that the attacker can carry out the breaking out free maneuver). The exercise can be changed further later e.g., so that the player with the puck in the neutral zone, after having done a feinting movement and a faked evading movement (against stands or cones), he ends up doing a wrist shot. Following this the player roles are changed over (see Diagram 28).

*Variation:*
- A second defending player intervenes from the red centerline after the finish of the 1:1 situation.

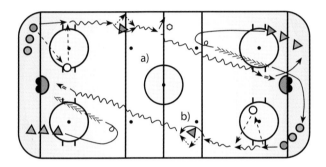

**Diagram 28**

Penetrating the attacking zone behind the blue line from along the boards can be done by carrying out an evading movement in the opposite direction. Breaking out free and a shot at goal or a pass can follow this action. In both cases, an increase in speed after the evading movement and good puck control are important throughout the whole action sequence. The attacking player has to convince the defender that he really intends to go down along the boards further into the game zone.

Another possibility is to feint a movement towards the boards followed by an evading movement into the center of the rink. If the opponent is not fast enough just behind the blue line, the player with the puck can play round him down the side nearest to the boards. At the moment that he comes with his body directly in front of the opponent, he tries to skate into the direction of the axis of the playing area and he can cover the puck with his body and the leg nearest to the opponent. The puck is normally dribbled along with a one-handed stick and the other arm is warding off the opponent's stick. It is important here, not to lose control of the puck and also to make sure that the action is completed by a shot at goal (see Diagram 29a).

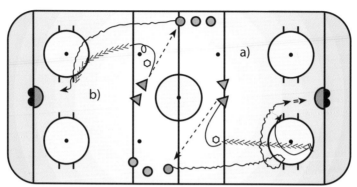

**Diagram 29**

As the last and most difficult example, included here is a solution for the 1:1 situation when skating out of the corner or from behind the goal mouth. First of all, exercises for the version of skating from the corner are covered where the attacker is facing frontally onto the playing area. Later on, we cover the situation where the player with the puck is skating with his back to the opponent and the playing area (see Diagram 30).

When doing the exercises, the defending player may, on no account, grapple with the attacker from behind with a lifted stick or with the hands (cross-checking, board-checking etc.). The player with the puck must have complete surety from the beginning that he will not be attacked in this way. Only this way will he be able to concentrate on using the correct technique. Training for this situation, however, should only be undertaken first of all when the players have mastered being able to break out free with the puck.

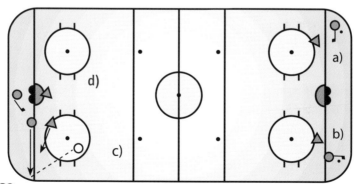

**Diagram 30**

## Methodical tips/Training emphasis

- Training for 1:1 situations is done, first of all, after mastering the individual breaking out free with the puck methods and after having firmed up the cycle; feinting – faking/evading movement – increase of speed.

- Particular note must be made of each individual player's ice-skating skills (backwards and forwards).

- The 1:1 situational exercises form the main technical and tactical emphasis for the training.

- All the exercises are carried out with regular changeovers of position. In this age group, there should be no emphasis on the roles and positions of attacker and defender.

- The trainer must explain the different variations and solutions (if needs be, he draws the sequences on a board or uses a video recording). It is advantageous when he also explains the advantages and disadvantages.

- The individual exercises can be done slowly at first by using stands and cones or other similar items.

- After mastering the basic technique, it is also possible to exercise using passive methods (without a stick, with reversed stick).

- Simple exercises are used for the training of tactics.

- To ensure that game play actions are internalized and become automatic, it is useful to carry out a second combined action, mainly in a different playing zone on the ice.

- The trainer should motivate the players to come up with creative solutions and make sure that they are repeated not just for the sake of doing repeats.

## 6.3 Breaking out Free without the Puck

From the viewpoint of systematic hockey training, here the subject is covered where a player breaks out free without the puck in order to place himself in an attacking position, having freed himself from a defender (moved into an unmarked position). This allows him to:

- To receive a pass and continue with the attacking play.
- To speed up the attacking play.
- To deliver a shot at goal after receiving the pass.
- To engage the opponent's attention, so that space is won for the player with the puck, as well as allowing other teammates, also without the puck, to be in a position to eventually join in the game play.
- To make a heavily occupied area less full and create additional free space.

A particular element of the actual practicing is that there should be regular changeovers of the role of attackers and defenders. Regarding the attack, the changes to be made should be concerning the actions done by the player without the puck. These actions speed up the play and also imply better opportunities for receiving a pass. Several players will then have the opportunity to develop an attacking action. Put in other words – the player without the puck who breaks out free is doing an individual action that gives the other attacking players better chances to develop that attack (its preparation, development and conclusion). In order to practice different combinations for the attack later, these actions should be given adequate attention by this age group.

Several factors and the interrelationship between them influence breaking free without the puck. Practice shows that the most important of these factors are:

- Ice-skating skills.
- The ability to receive a pass (on the move, under pressure, in a confined space, receiving an inaccurate pass etc.).
- The ability to be able to "read" the game (anticipation).
- The different areas on the ice and the playing zones (defending and neutral zones, the area along the boards, on the central axis of the rink, the area in front of the opposing goal mouth, the areas round the blue lines (defense and attack) etc.).
- Covering and marking variations (open or close marking, between the opponent and own goal or between the opponent and the puck or the opponent without the puck).
- Combination play by players without the puck moving about.
- The team's game system.

The first factor that influences breaking out free without the puck is ice-skating ability and skills. Rapid changes of movement, skating into tight and wide curves and increasing speed, turns, starts and stops all form essential requirements for success in these individual attack actions. A good ice-skater can master all changes of direction in a confined space without dropping his speed and losing a firm posture and his overview. The skating action is also hindered by the defensive actions of the opponent (marking). Additionally, the requirement to keep the blade of the stick always in contact with the ice (or just above the surface) ready to make a pass, makes ice-skating more difficult. Regarding ice-skating skills, breaking out free without the puck, is done by:

- changing direction.
- changing speed, as well as,
- a combination of changes in direction and speed – by maneuvering.

The attacking players have to learn that they must always be on the move and never stand still. Even the player, who is moving around slowly has better chances to be able to make a quick change of position than the one who stands still. Looking at the whole action, the push-off starting movement creates better conditions for receiving the puck and then dribbling with it as well as increasing speed. Marking and covering the attacking player is considerably more difficult when seen from the defender's point of view. To a certain extent the player's energy potential is not used to the full. Speed and the direction without the puck depend on the game situation at the time. In play, we are speaking about a lateral (sideways) movement, a movement in the opposite direction, a linear (straight ahead) movement and about skating into and out of curves. To complete everything, there is also the diagonal forwards movement (see Diagram 31). Considering the tactical variations, when organizing team play for the attack, there will be situations where the attacker will remain skating alongside the boards (for example when building up an attack in the defending zone).

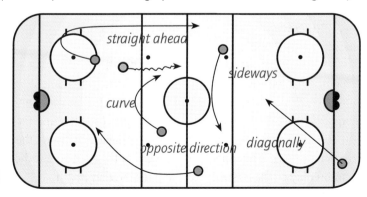

**Diagram 31**

In play without the puck, not only is one player able to free himself, all the others are also freed into clear space. The movements of the player without the puck are not only done with due regard to the position of the player with the puck, but also to the positions of all the other players, who also do not have the puck. The positions of the opponents in defense play an equally important role (defense tactics). Corresponding movements, constant changes of position in the free spaces and combined play, all done by the players without the puck increase the probability of being able to receive a pass better (see Diagram 32). Besides this, the player without the puck, who frees himself from the opposition and draws him with him, creates an opening for the player with the puck (see Diagram 33).

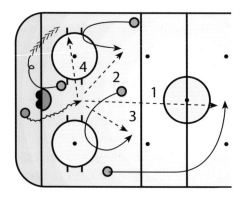

**Diagram 32**

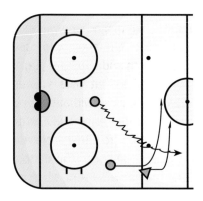

**Diagram 33**

This proves to young players that they should not position themselves where their teammates already are. A swarm of attackers in a confined space is actually advantageous to the defending team.

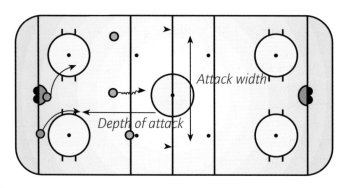

**Diagram 34**

Only sufficient staggering of the depth and width within the whole of the attacking action will give a surety for a successful outcome (see Diagram 34). The exceptions will be game situations where good marking, cross shots and short supporting passes are employed. By this, attacking actions in front of the opposing goal (when shooting or playing to outnumber the opposition) as well as practiced game play moves (for example breaking free out of the corner by using 2-3 players), are meant. These types of solution are described first of all for older age groups.

All of the movements and positioning of the players without the puck should make it possible for the attacker with the puck to pass it, while at the same time guaranteeing a suitable defensive posture in case the puck is lost. It is important that the players advance in a triangular formation (the attacking triangle – two attackers forward with one trailing up behind or vice-versa) mainly in the neutral and in the attacking zones. The triangular formation, with good visual control of the puck all round, provides sufficient width and depth for play, not only in the build-up of the attack, but also what follows, providing that there is corresponding play organized in the defense.

Breaking out free without the puck in the attacking zone is different from breaking out free in the defending and neutral zones. This can be seen in the different aims of the attacking action (to either score a goal or at least threaten the goal by creating fresh shooting opportunities). The attacking team, in particular, has the more difficult task, because the game is taking place in a confined space (in the zone there are 10 players) and the defender is (naturally) concentrating on defending. In this situation, the players without the puck have to unmark themselves from the opposing players by doing rapid changes of direction and feinting movements. They must be able to receive the puck when under pressure and deliver shots at goal or pass to players in a better position. In the shooting zone, the players leave it to the last moment to break away free, so that the opposition finds difficulty in marking. The players with and without the puck have to be able to "read" the game and anticipate the next playing action well. They do this while at the same time keeping on the move and doing frequent feinting maneuvers.

The players without the puck in the attacking zone have to always consider defense (in case of loss of the puck). The trainer must drill in the requirement for the triangular formation (one player is always on the move or is in the area of the blue attacking line – see Diagram 35). Young players should not yet be bothered with the question of who has to act as the back-up (last man) player. In practice, the player who is farthest away from the puck assumes the position as the first defender. Besides this, the players should be ready to back up the actions of the other teammates and come up with creative solutions for the various game situations together. The advantage of the triangular formation is the ability to place the opponent under pressure (forechecking). This is shown in the situation where the attacking team loses the puck (two players nearest to the puck attack immediately and the third attacker – furthest away from the puck – assumes the task of a drawn back attacker in a defending position).

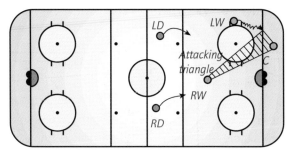

RD – Right defenseman    LW – Left winger
LD – Left defenseman     C – Center
RW – Right winger

**Diagram 35**

The aim in breaking away free without the puck is to achieve a better position to receive a pass. Without this, the attacking action cannot be successful. A requirement for this is a clean receipt of the pass and follow-on action (shot at goal, dribbling the puck on and breaking out free or making a pass). For this age group, the playing action is the uppermost thing, with consideration being given to how to receive the puck in realistic game-like situations. In practice, the technique as well as the tactics should be practiced. The players should always make sure that they are positioned sideways or frontally to the player with the puck, and at the same time they must keep an eye on the movements of the defenders and their own teammates. The players should get used to steering towards such areas where they can receive a pass ("offer themselves up for a pass"). To start with, the trainer should not tolerate when a player without the puck takes up a position where he is not able to actively take part in the attack. In practice, this is about situations where the player without the puck, at the moment when the pass occurs, is "hidden" behind the opponent or turns his back on his teammate with the puck.

Individual exercises are done, to start with, without any opposition. The passive obstacles represented by equipment (cones and stands) play an important role here. The trainer can make the area where the action is to take place narrower (e.g., the area where the pass is due to be taken on). When the player without the puck breaks free, he has to get into the zone, where he wants to receive the puck, rapidly. His speed will make it difficult for the defender to mark him. Before he receives the pass, the player has to anticipate what he will do next ("read" the game), because he will have no time for this later. The next diagram shows an example of receiving a pass with a follow-up action (dribbling, passing and feinting maneuvers with a fake) using cones. The exercise is done on a signal and is practiced in both directions.

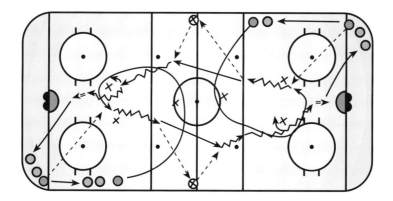

**Diagram 36**

As has already been mentioned, the direction a player takes can be linear, in the opposite direction, lateral or curved. Training must cover all these situations when practicing puck control (see Diagram 37). Furthermore, the player must be able to bring the puck under control in situations where for example there is an inaccurate pass (bounces off the skate, too far forward or to the rear etc.), or after passes where the puck lifts up off the ice or is in the air. There are exercises for taking the puck pass on with the hand and for passes when holding the stick in one hand.

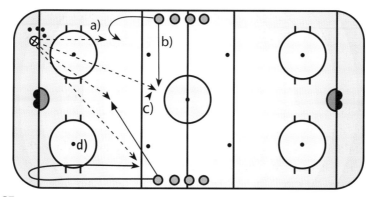

**Diagram 37**

The effectiveness of play by the player without the puck depends on correctly judging the game situation – "reading" the game and inputting the necessary actions. Execution of the right movement and giving up a good pass is dependent on good "timing", which is essential.

In order to get the correct timing, it is necessary that the player increases acceleration at the correct moment and chooses the correct angle. The player without the puck has to be able to "read' the play so that at the moment when the pass is made, he is in the optimum position to receive the pass and build up play further or bring the attack to a conclusion. Correct timing with rapid movement in a forward direction considerably increases the player's chance to complete the intended action. The young players have to learn to fit into their environment and space. Breaking out free into a space where he will be able to collect the pass at the correct moment is exactly what is required to be successful. The player without the puck can influence the timing, either by changing the path he takes (he shortens or lengthens the movement to the spot where he expects the pass) or his speed. The change of path and speed, coupled with a feinting movement makes it possible for him to get unmarked. For practicing this, the selection of the exercise should concentrate on both variations, or, better still, combine them. An increase in speed for the pass must, however, be underlined (see Diagram 38).

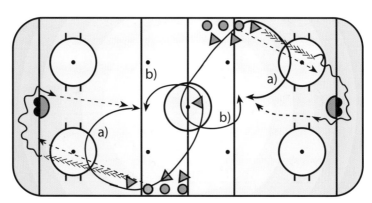

**Diagram 38**

The fine tuning of the timing, when the player breaks free, must not be seen as the only movement he has to make. What we are talking about here is a combination of the individual movements, with the aim of enabling as many chances as possible for any one of the players in the triangular formation (with adequate width and depth in

the attacking action) to receive a pass. The player, who is constantly on the move, fixates the opponent, thus making more room for his teammates, one with the puck. The constant dodging backwards and forwards also gives him room to be in a position to take a pass.

In training, one, two or three players should practice the timing exercises together. The next diagram shows an example for a timing exercise with one and three players without introducing an opponent into the practice. The main emphasis for the exercise is either in judging the speed of the movements or the length of the path taken.

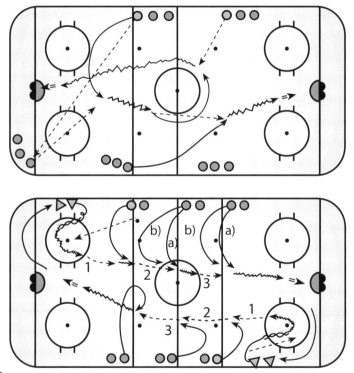

**Diagram 39**

The principle of changing position is also part of the business of breaking free. This means that the player without the puck moves into the position, which his teammate has just vacated. Included in the combinations that are based on this principle is the action of crossing and drop passing the puck. In keeping with the ice-hockey system of training these are play combinations that will be explained later.

These playing actions constitute the basis for cooperation by the players in the attack. It is not only a question of combinations being played by two or three players, but the cooperation of all five. When training for the breakaway by the player without the puck, it must be understood that this is a basis for the build-up of the attack in all the playing zones. The exercises for this must be selected in a manner that the players can practice the slow and fast build-up of the attack. In practice, this means that the preparatory and game exercises cover the short and long passes in the various playing zones.

## Methods

### Tips for technique training

- The player breaking away moves into the free space diagonally, in a curve (both skating forwards and backwards), always in a sideways or frontal posture to his teammate with the puck.

- The correct timing must be concentrated on from the beginning.

- The stick blade, which must be held always on the ice (or just above it), is angled correctly in anticipation of leading the puck on.

- The player must be able to master various different ways of receiving the puck and puck control (inaccurate pass, flat, high, drop catching with the hand etc.).

- The player breaking away must learn to keep his eye on the player with the puck, the opponent and his own teammates, all at the same time.

- After receiving a puck pass, it is important that further playing actions are practiced – breaking out free with the puck, shooting and passing.

All ice-skating exercises are suitable as preparatory exercises. Further to this, various game forms and exercising in pairs (chasing games, copy cat games), as well as exercises practicing changing directions are also used.

First of all, in training the simplest starting movements (straight forward, diagonal, and in a curve) are practiced and later the more complicated ones are covered (entering the curve with a changeover to backwards skating up through to changing postures). The basic movement is straight ahead and progresses into a diagonal movement (see Diagrams 40 and 41).

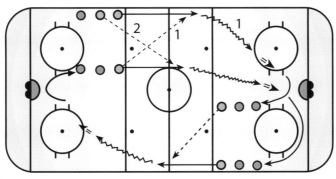

**Diagram 40**

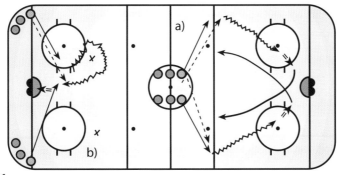

**Diagram 41**

Additionally, starting and breaking away skating into a curve forwards is practiced. Tight curves, with exits from them, as well as curves done using the cross-over step, are important. The main emphasis lies in increasing speed in the curve and rapid exits from them. For reasons of a methodical nature, curves done in the direction of the boards should also be practiced, and not only ones into the center of the playing area (see Diagram 42).

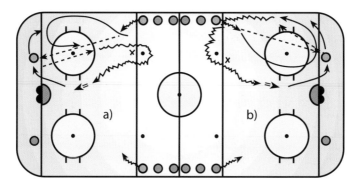

**Diagram 42**

Training should also include exercises, where a player has to start by moving laterally. Later, more complicated variations should be practiced – by exiting a curve forwards and then moving over to a backwards skating motion. All the exercises can be finished with a shot at goal, or with a direct pass. The exercises all consist principally of actions to do turns, stops, starts forwards and backwards. Training is done first of all without any opposition, with conditions being made more difficult later. For this purpose, cones are useful (to limit the area where the pass takes place). The next diagram shows an exercise example where a player starts off into a curve, changes over to skating backwards, receives a pass, changes back to skating forwards and succeeds in a 1:1 situation. In the other variation (see Diagram 43b), a turn and the combination of passing as you skate is practiced after the start. The action is concluded with a shot at goal. The players then change over positions.

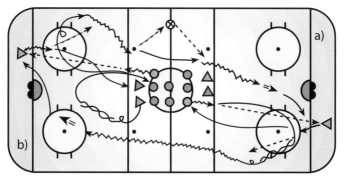

**Diagram 43**

A basic element of the starting exercises for practicing the long pass is the correct timing, with the possibility to change the path taken and the speed (see Diagram 44).

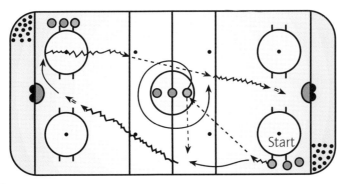

**Diagram 44**

Other important exercises are those dealing with practicing anticipation where there are several players (2-3) involved. The player with the puck tries out various ways. It is advantageous, if he does the exercise from a predetermined zone where he should offer up the pass. In this way, the players without the puck are forced to have to "read" the play to get into the position where they will pick up the pass and continue on with the attacking action. The exercises are done without any opposition, or with different levels of opposition, (e.g., three players breakaway to receive a pass and one, two or three players do the marking) (see Diagram 45). The players (in threes or fours) change over positions when the exercise action is finished. After a pass or a shot at goal, two players start off trying to judge the best path and speed. The players try to conclude the action 2:0. The defending player tries to reach the two players and hinder the shot. The exercise is done from both sides alternately.

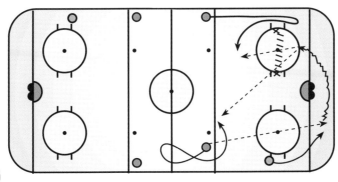

**Diagram 45**

In the training system, we follow now with the next game exercise, in which the player without the puck breaks out free from the opponent. It is recommended to do the exercises in an outnumbered situation 1+1:1; 1+2:2 or directly begin using situations with 2:1 and 3:2. The player with the puck then has more time to pass it to the player breaking out (see Diagram 46).

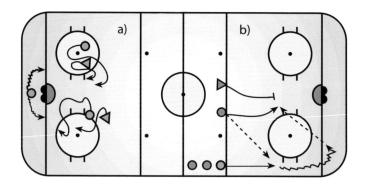

**Diagram 46**

Exercises for breaking out are then only finally practiced in situations 2:2; 3:3; 4:4 and 5:5 and various degrees of opposition (the players taking part do so without sticks or with sticks reversed etc.). The exercises are done in all the various playing zones. The next diagram shows a breakaway in a 2:2 and a 3:3 situation. The trainer starts the action with a face-off in different areas of the playing zone. The two players nearest the puck overcome a 1:1 situation. For other pairs, the participants break out free to receive a pass and end the action with a shot, or try to pass the puck to a teammate in a better position.

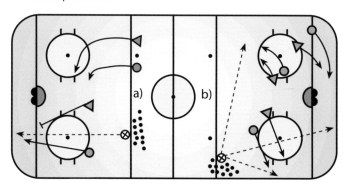

**Diagram 47**

## Methodical tips/Training emphasis

- An important requirement for training of these playing moves is a perfect skating technique, mainly being able to skate out of tight and broad curves, do turns, and starting and stopping.
- The basic variations are practiced using static aids (stands, cones). The trainer watches to make sure that all players practice the breakaway.
- Various preparatory exercises are done in pairs (also the defense – covering by the player without the puck).
- Training should take place in the playing zones where these actions actually happen during a game.
- The players gradually learn to move jointly (i.e., they take note of what the other players (with or without the puck) are doing.
- Step by step, playing against opposition is increased in intensity.
- When the players can master the game actions, situations 1+1:2, 1+2:2, 2:2, 3:3 are practiced where the breakaway player is given a pass (while at the same time, the defense is practiced – covering by the player without the puck).
- The players must get used to being constantly on the move while in the free areas.
- A difference is made between exercises for breaking out free during the build-up of the attack and exercises for developing the attack and finishing off an attack.
- All exercises with opposing players participating also brings another individual action into the game – covering by the player without the puck.

## Main mistakes

- The player doesn't try to break away from the opponent (no increase in speed, no feinting movement).
- The player breaking free is always behind the opponent.
- Incorrect timing of the movement stops the pass coming in.
- Simultaneous and coordinating movements are absent in all of the players without the puck.
- When skating off, starting, the player doesn't check his teammates (with and without the puck).
- When skating off, starting, the player doesn't check where the opponent is (danger of injury).
- Speed is insufficient when breaking away from the opponent.
- Before a pass is given, the blade of the stick is not on the ice or only a few centimeters above the ice.
- After breaking out free and receiving a pass, the player stops without getting back into the game.
- The players all break out free in the same direction without varying it.

## 6.4 Shooting Training

The basic shooting techniques, together with methodical tips, have already been covered in the book "Hockey – First Steps for Kids". Some of the shot variations (e.g., the slap shot) should be learned first of all when they reach the 9 and 10 year old age group. In spite of this, in the following section we will cover further aspects, which are often decisive for the outcome of competitions. These deal with shots taken in the immediate vicinity of the goal and actions after the shot (intentional fake shots (tip-in), rebound shots and blocking the goalie's visibility).

**Shots immediately in front of the goal**

In training, in all age groups, considerable time should be devoted to practicing shots that are made in the immediate vicinity of the goal and are specific actions. Goal shooting skills play an important role and are decisive with regard to a team's success or failure. Training for this is never-ending, so therefore, as a theme it is always being mentioned.

After finishing training the attack actions, the young players should begin once they have mastered the basic techniques of the wrist and full shots as well as the forehand and backhand versions.

The effectiveness of a shot is not only dependent on technical and tactical factors, but also on psychological and fitness factors. Concentration and space orientation for this has to be taught to young players. When a player is in front of the goal, he has to try to hide his intention from the goalie and defenders. This will be dependent on the skill to break out free quickly, take on a pass and, without any build-up, shoot straight away. Success will only come from a flexible, well-aimed, surprise shot. The speed of the shot depends on the rapid stroke of the stick blade. In these situations, the combination of strength (mainly concerning how heavy the defense is mounted) and the strength of the parts of the body (arms, rear, shoulders, legs etc.) is important. Maintaining a good posture in a shooting position will also make the player's action more successful. In these type of game actions, determination and speed exercised, when receiving any kind of pass, both play a big role (knocking down the high pass with the stick blade or the hand, the skate, the body etc.,) in the final result. After making the shot, the player watches his puck and stays in the shooting area in case he can score from a rebound.

The most common shooting techniques used in the immediate vicinity of the goal are:

## Forehand shots

- Wrist shot.
- Full shot.
- Without any build-up.
- "With a 'long' stick (stick held out with the puck further from the body).
- Playing round a goalie on the floor or over his stick.
- With the tip of the blade.
- A push shot into goal after skating round it.
- A shot taken out of a turn.
- When falling down or in a kneeling, sitting, lying position.
- Knocking the puck down out of the air with the stick blade.

**Backhand shots** – similar techniques as in the forehand shots.

## Shooting with the stick held in only one hand

## Correct technique and practical tips

- Keep the head upright.
- Watch the goalie.
- Keep the stick blade down on the ice.
- Follow through.
- Remain in the shooting area (in order to score from a rebound).

In practice, it has been found useful if the young players remember these actions from short made-up sayings.

For example:
- The aim is not necessarily just to shoot at goal, it is to score a goal.
- The player has to shoot at goal, but only when the goalie is out of range.
- The close-quarter shot must be done rapidly and hard.
- Only the player, who tries hard, will score a goal.
- In front of the goal, the blade of the stick must always be on the ice.
- The action is not over until the referee blows his whistle.

## Methodical tips/Training emphasis

- The shots should be done without a lot of lining up or preparation – or only giving sufficient time for a pass to be received.
- The player tries to shoot the puck into the open goal (normally into the upper and lower corners, between the goalie's legs or from an angle into the long corner (by the goal mouth post).
- If the shot follows a pass, the puck must be played as quickly as possible.
- Passes in front of the goal mouth should be directed out of various different angles.
- The player finishes off the shot action with a technique, which doesn't require a large pulling back of the stick (use a flip shot or a wrist shot). Another variation is to make sure that the blade is angled correctly (correct lie) so that a fake shot can be carried out.
- Practice shooting on the forehand and the backhand.
- At the beginning use simple exercises and then move on to the more complex ones.
- Use several skills one after the other: Shoot several pucks at goal, one after the other.
- Coordination practice: Between shots at goal, carry out other actions (turning, jumping over hurdles, kneeling down etc.).
- Limit the shooting time: The passes come in quickly one after the other and only after a certain period may the defender join in.
- Space limitations: The player may only use a specific sector to shoot from.
- The player may not stand around in the sector.
- Cones are erected in front of the goal, which the player must not hit or touch.
- Technical limitations: The player may only use one particular type of shot.
- After shooting, always follow the puck with your eyes – rebound possible.
- After a teammate has shot at goal, always follow the puck with your eyes in case there is a possibility to perform a fake shot or a rebound shot.
- All actions are done, first of all without any opposition, the emphasis being on speed and timing of decisions – later they are carried out in tight areas under pressure with other players joining in.
- These exercises should be a part of every session for all age groups.

Training for shooting practice should be done on the whole area of the rink. Where possible, a goalie can also take part. Watch for the change of positions and change of direction for passing (see Diagram 48).

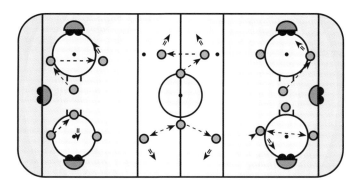

**Diagram 48**

Practicing for high shots is done by delivering five shots, one after the other over a player lying down (the goalie) or over a hurdle (see Diagram 49). Approaching the goal should be done with adequate speed and against an opponent (see Diagram 50).

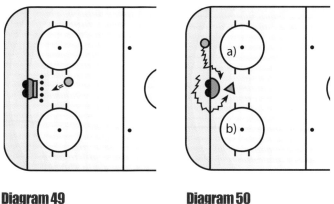

**Diagram 49**          **Diagram 50**

Diagram 51a shows a shot following a pass from the side by the boards. The players are divided up into groups of three where each one shoots two pucks with a change of position. By practicing a quick shot after a pass out of a variety of directions, the player learns to be able to orient himself and follow the movements of the puck and the goalie (see Diagram 51).

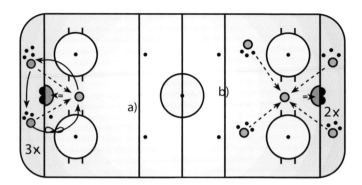

**Diagram 51**

Exercises, carried out often where the players have to bring play to an end with actions under pressure of time and space, make superb model examples that they will bound to be used in a proper game. Take this as an example: After a turn, the attacker receives a pass, carries out a feinting movement with a fake against a cone (passive opposition) and then shoots. A second pass then comes in and a second shot is made. The next puck is taken on from behind the goal net by the player, who skates round in front of the goal or he pushes the puck into the goal (see Diagram 52).

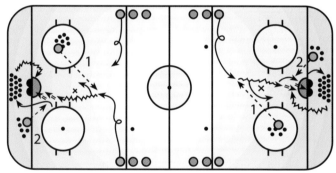

**Diagram 52**

The exercises are carried out first of all using various aids (stands, cones etc.). The players are then made to do other exercises just prior to ending the movement in order to practice their agility – turns, kneeling down and jumping). An example is shown in Diagram 53. The player dribbles the puck along, jumps over a hurdle and shoots at goal. There is then another hurdle to be overcome and this is followed up by a second pass and a quick finish.

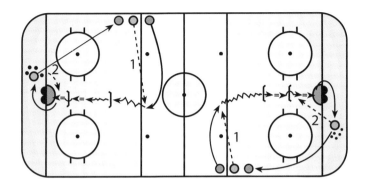

**Diagram 53**

Diagram 54 shows an action where a pass is carried out in front of the goal with a defender in the way. The player breaks out free to take on the pass by making a quick change of direction and a feint so that one of his two teammates can bring him into play.

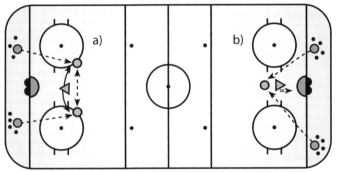

**Diagram 54**

### After the shot

In addition to the game actions in front of the goal, there are also actions to be done after the shot.
In practice, both in training and in competition, a difference is made as follows:

- Intentional fake shot (tip-in).
- Shooting in a rebound shot (the second shot).
- Obscure or limit the goalie's vision.

In the game these days, which is characterized by a well organized defense and a rapid, aggressive attack on the player with the puck, the opportunities to prepare for a shot (full shot) are limited. In a game 5:5, in the attacking zone or in an outnumbered situation 5:4, a surprise wrist shot or a puck pass across the front of the goal mouth is more effective when dealing with an aggressive defense.

Generally speaking, any action taken after doing a shot will increase its effectiveness and at the same time reduce the goalie's chances to save. Learning these playing actions is not difficult, but it does demand that the player has the guts to always stay in contact with the opponent. Furthermore, the player requires good strength and technical skills and be able to judge the situation well. By repeating these actions often, the young players gain confidence in being able to do the sequences in front of the goal, and are then able to carry out important and effective play after the shot at goal. Because of this, each training session should not only include shooting practice but also follow up shots and actions.

### Intentional fake shot with the puck

The intentional fake shot with the puck is an individual game action where the player tries to change the flight of the puck. This activity is carried out in front of (next to) the goal or when entering the area at the moment that the shot is delivered. The player stands in front of (or next to) the goalie in the basic position and is facing the teammate with the blade of his stick on the ice (see Diagram 55).

**Diagram 55**

Another variation is when the attacker is alongside the goal mouth and the blade of his stick is pointing in the direction, in which the shooter will deliver the shot. The attacker tries to deflect the puck with the blade (eventually also by using a part of his body). The sudden change of direction of the puck makes defense by the goalie difficult. It often leads to a rebound, which can be shot at goal again.

A more difficult variation of the intentional fake is where the player passes into a clear area where his teammate takes on the pass. The teammate moves into this position in anticipation of the play coming up. This version is normally practiced later on in the older age groups.

The puck shots should slide over the ice or be only just a little above the surface. The intentional fake (deflection) carries no risks and is simpler and more accurate. Confidence in the player doing the move relies very much in the readiness to get into a good open position in front of the goal. This point is very important particularly in young players. Assurance that you won't get hit gradually grows and firms up the proper way of getting into the goal area at the correct moment the pass comes in. The player's position in front of the goal when the intentional tip-in takes place, is similar to the position where the player tries to obscure the goalie's sight and the correct method makes the play action more effective.

## Rebound shots

In play nowadays, this action is tremendously important from the viewpoint of the goalie. This is not a technically complicated action. It is often accompanied by a fake with the puck and hindering the goalie's vision. Nevertheless, it demands split-second reaction, determination, personal courage and the ability to keep the eye on the puck and the goalie while getting into position. Because the action takes place in a confined space in front of the opponent's goal, good orientation coupled with adequate strength are important.

In training, the same game principles are used as in the actions for doing the intentional fake deflection and obscuring the goalie's vision. When doing a rebound shot there is no particular shooting technique used. Generally, you use either a quick wrist shot or a forehand or backhand flip shot from a variety of positions (standing, sitting, kneeling, as you fall down etc.). The player's attitude in doing this shot is important. It is advantageous to have the blade of the stick touching the surface of the ice. Included in this version is where the shot rebounds off the backboards (behind the goal) and is shot in off this rebound. It is, however, recommended that practice for this version takes place later.

The basics of the rebound shot and the tip-in and the exercises best used to practice these are summarized as follows:

- When concluding the attack build-up, the scheme is to have at least one player in front of the opponent's goal (the triangular formation).
- The player doing the tip-in has to be facing or standing sideways on to the teammate dribbling the puck and make sure that he is unmarked.
- The tip-in and the rebound shot can be done either in front of or alongside the goal mouth.
- Being able to start skating into the area in front of the goal just at the moment the shot is delivered is very effective, because this makes it difficult for the opponents to mark.
- The player doing the shot aims at the blade of the teammate for the tip-in.
- Always attempt to do these shots (whether coming across over the ice or just above it) for any puck shot.
- When the attacker is on his own (no teammate present) in front of the opponent's goal, the shot should be delivered with as much strength as possible assuming that the goalie has his eye on the puck (situation 1:0; 1:1 etc.).
- In various different tactics, the backboards behind the goal can be used to deliver a second shot by rebounding the puck off the boards.

**Obscuring the goalie's vision**
The aim of this action is to hinder the goalie's concentration by obscuring his vision. The player doing the action takes up a basic stance, facing the dribbling teammate. He is in between his teammate and the goalie, so that the latter cannot see either the puck or the attacking player (see Diagram 56).

**Diagram 56**

The attacker stands firmly on both legs with knees well bent directly in front of the goalie (however, the rule regarding the position of the goalie (in the goal crease) must be observed). Besides this, it is advantageous when he, within the rules, constantly attacks the goalie's stick. This action makes it difficult for the goalie to catch and save flat shots over the ice and hinders his concentration considerably. Efficient control of the stick gives the attacker more opportunities to do a shot (against cleared shots or rebounds).

The attacker's concentration and observation of the goalie, his stick and the puck all play an important role. The player, when engaged in front of the goal, is in the center of the other team's defensive play, not only by defensemen but also the goalie. Personal courage and guts are important and also, for older age groups, strength and fitness. The trainer should praise the players often when they complete successful moves.

## Methodical tips

- Basic training must cover mastering all the shooting variations.
- After every shot at goal, at least one of the three moves following a shot has to be practiced.
- Prior to the training session, a comprehensive description and a practical demonstration of the move sequences should be given.
- First of all, exercises are carried out without a goalie and slow, flat shots, which slide over the ice should be used.
- A goalie is then brought on, and slow, flat shots, which slide over the ice, should be used again.
- Exercises with fast shots (which slide over the ice or lift up a little).
- Practice game situations with a defending player.
- Practicing the movements particularly in situations on the move (move in front of the goal at the moment the shot comes in).

In training, first of all, simple exercises (with emphasis on doing the correct movement sequences) are done and then, later, more complicated variations (with an opponent and sequences after a start) are carried out. For these exercises, the skills learned to date should be worked at.

Before practicing the tip-in techniques and rebound shots from a passed puck, here are some exercises (see Diagram 57).

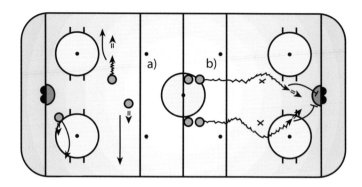

**Diagram 57**

In the next diagram, exercises in the basic position for all the actions after a teammate's shot (tip-in, rebound shots, obscuring the vision) are illustrated. It is important that the player stands facing or sideways to the attacker and that the stick blade is touching the ice. The players changeover in pairs after five shots. Another organizational variation is where two (three) players shoot at goal, one after the other. When doing the tip-in, it should be practiced on the forehand as well as on the backhand. Where possible, the goalie should be included in play.

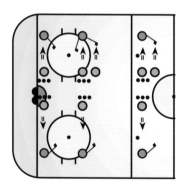 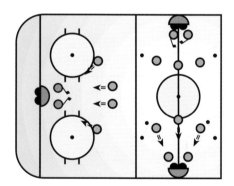

**Diagram 58**

Variations with exercises for 1:1; 2:0; 1:1 etc., follow where the player goes after the puck when it has been shot and stops in front of the goal (see Diagram 59). The player is now required to do exactly the same action as his teammate, who passes to him for the shot. In this way, the player is forced to have to start from in front of the goal and become involved in play. It is important that the player stands facing or sideways to the attacker and that the stick blade is touching the ice. This exercise, with an opponent playing, can help to develop strength (see Diagram 60).

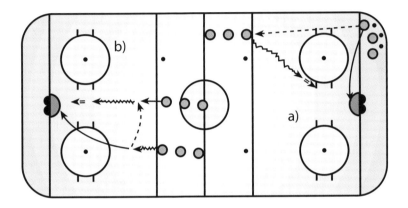

**Diagram 59**

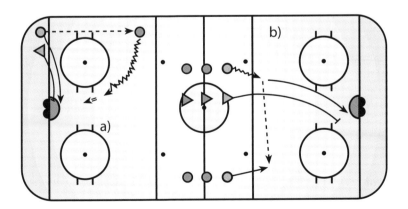

**Diagram 60**

The next diagram shows an exercise for the rebound shot following up an attempt at a shot. Then, a teammate does a shot with a tip-in and a rebound shot. At the moment the shot comes in, the player doing the tip-in must stand facing or sideways to the player executing the shot.

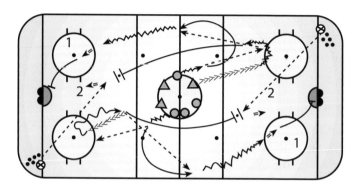

**Diagram 61**

**Main Mistakes**

- The player doesn't skate round in front of the goal after the shot.
- Wrong positioning by the player.
- The player is standing passively in front of the goal and doesn't obscure the goalie's vision.
- The player misses the puck.
- The player doesn't follow the path of the puck.
- No commitment to push the rebound shot into the goal (no will to score).
- The stick blade is not touching the ice.
- The player is standing with his back towards the player executing the shot (danger of injury).
- The player doesn't tip-in the puck and score (wrong sense of direction).
- An overactive player skates into the goal area and attacks the goalie unfairly (feeling for space).

# 7 Defense Strategy

A s already mentioned in a previous chapter, the team in defense does not have the puck under control. The main aim is to avoid a goal being scored or that the defense comes under pressure. Possession of the puck must be regained and brought under control again. Puck possession depends on:

- The individual technical and tactical skills of the player, as well as,
- The tactical performance of the whole team.

A constant switch between attack and defense, nowadays, characterizes play. By working at the defense, the changeover to an attacking situation is actually already achieved. The whole organization of a team's game in defense is built on the demands of moving into the attack and vice-versa.

The success of a team is guaranteed by players who have a feeling and sufficient commitment for playing without a puck. All the players should be versed in the principles of defense in all the playing zones and at the same time in all playing positions. Defense play mirrors the morale of the whole team. The trainer should not underestimate the good players and he should never tolerate incorrect defense play. The effectiveness of the whole team in the defense is dependent on the ability of the weakest player in defense. The mastering of the techniques for individual playing actions is an important requirement of any tactic. As long as ice-skating techniques, marking the players with the puck (attacking, tackling and puck possession) and marking players without the puck have all not been learned properly, it is not worth while beginning to do training for defense combinations and defense systems.

In the 9-10 year age group, the players learn how to use their bodies and how they can win tackling fights. Therefore, skills are preferable where they cover tackling and gaining possession of the puck or where outnumbering is achieved. Nevertheless, it must be said that performance in this age group is not based on tackling fights with heavy body checking. There will be enough time for this when the children's strength is better developed (at the end of puberty). At the moment, however, the main emphasis is particularly on ice-skating skills, on the movements to be used when attacking and the technical skills of handling a pass with the stick. Tackling fights can be seen rather more as an additional titbit to brighten up and complement the training session.

Nevertheless, these kind of playing actions will be described here so that the methods and systems are covered. The trainer can then select those skills that are appropriate for the age group in his class. Of course, he will take account of the technical and tactical abilities they possess.

## 7.1   Marking the Player with the Puck

Marking the player with the puck means carrying out the defense with the aim of regaining possession of the puck or slowing down the speed of the attacking action, and above all to push the opponent into a more favorable area where the defenders can operate more freely with further defense in mind. This action is called checking.

In addition to using this term generally, there are also two other forms of checking. Forechecking is when the defenders tackle the other team and attempt to take the puck away in the other team's half of the rink. Backchecking is trying to take the puck away with the defenders in their own half of the rink.

Checking the opponent, who has the puck, is the essential element of the whole of the defense game. The effectiveness of this action is the decider of any game success. Checking has three important functions:
- To get the puck back under control.
- To take the puck off the opponent.
- To reduce the speed of the attack, thus allowing a teammate to get back and assist in marking the opponent.

Checking is just as important for the defense as stickhandling and dribbling is for the attack. As already mentioned, good ice-skating technique is an important prerequisite. The technique as a whole, with all of its components – skating speed, agility (coordination), balance and power – belongs to the main prerequisites for all individual defense actions.

Before defense play is described, it should be mentioned that the same principles apply for defense play in all the playing zones:
- The nearest player to the opponent dribbling with the puck is the first player, who checks that opponent (unless something else has been agreed beforehand, he should check the opponent straight away).
- Defense effort should be concentrated down the central axis of the rink, with the opponents being forced out towards the boards.
- The defending player should maintain an optimum defensive position on the ice i.e., between the opponent and his own goal or between the opponent with the puck and one without the puck.
- The defender's actions must prevent the opponent passing to his teammate or receiving a pass from a teammate.
- Marking the opponent is done, according to situation and space, either by marking the man or controlling space.
- The aim of any defense action is to reduce the speed of the opponent's attack and

control the attack this way. Besides this, the attackers of the defending team must be able to overtake their opposing attackers by skating back into their own defending zone (backchecking) and assuming a defensive position there.
- Keep talking with teammates (cooperation and support).
- If the defender is too slow or is too far away from an opponent, he should switch over to marking an area.

When marking a player with the puck (or one without the puck), the position of the defender in relation to the opponent and to his own goal must be watched. Depending, there are two forms of marking:
- Marking between the opponent with the puck and goal being defended (see Diagram 62).
- Marking between the opponent with the puck and an opponent without the puck (see Diagram 63).

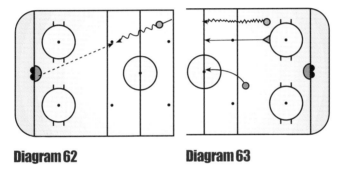

**Diagram 62**          **Diagram 63**

The type of marking to be used has to be selected with reference to the playing zone and playing space. Marking in one's own half takes place mainly between the opponent with the puck and the home goal. Besides this, tactics and positioning (defender/attacker) will have an influence on the method selected for any particular situation.

When marking a player, with or without the puck, the distance between the defending player and the opponent will also play an important role. We speak, here, of two further variations of marking:
- Open marking – marking an area.
- Tight or close marking – marking the man.

For open marking, the defending player is not in direct contact with the opponent. The term **contact**, used here, means physical contact as well as stick contact. In play nowadays, where the puck is mainly in the attacking half of the rink, open marking is used – by passive (control of space or delaying tactics) checking and in situations where they are outnumbered.

A characteristic feature of hockey today is the rapid checking of the opponent with the puck by using close marking. Close marking is used whenever the distance between the defending player and the opponent is less than the length of the hockey stick. Closing with the opponent and the tackling play that follows provides the initial prerequisite for regaining possession of the puck. Therefore, when the puck has been lost, young players in this age group should move to check the attack straight away. It is the duty of every defender to mark the man with the puck in his own half (above all when the defensive zone has been penetrated).

A basic situation, where man marking of the player with the puck needs to be resolved, is an even-balanced 1:1 situation. The solution can be found for all and any of the playing zones and areas, while at the same time the skating skills of the checking player will play a big role in this. Checking the player with the puck consists of the following actions:
- Closing with the opponent.
- Carrying out a tackle.
- Taking the puck away from him.
- Carrying out fair body-checking.

If the defender is not able to get in close contact with the opponent with the puck, then the checking movements consist of the following actions:
- First of all, skating towards the opponent.
- Then close with the opponent for contact.
- Tackling actions.
- Taking away the puck.

When tackling, use of the body is made. Diagram 64 shows the individual actions in the checking action, irrespective of whether the defending player is skating forwards or backwards or is chasing after the attacker.

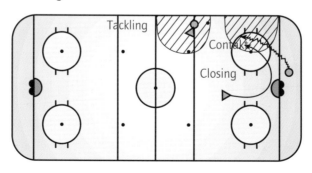

**Diagram 64**

## 'Closing into contact'

This term means that the defender chases after the opponent and closes with him. One differentiates for the whole of this action between the speed and pressure placed on the opponent with the puck and the variation of ice-skating skills used by the defending checker. There are two different methods used according to speed and pressure:

- Passive checking – area marking (without body contact with the opponent).
- Aggressive checking – closing with the opponent rapidly and harassing him.

The first player carrying out the checking action will decide which variation of checking is used. This player is usually the player nearest to the opponent attacking – that is, provided that there is no other tactical aspect to play). The player makes his decision on the basis of how he sees the game developing and in line with certain principles that the trainer will have described to the youngest age group.

Aggressive checking is mainly used where:

- The checking player has already closed contact with or is close to the opponent dribbling the puck
- The opponent with the puck has turned his back to the checking player.
- The opponent has lost control of the puck.
- The opponent with the puck is on his own and there is no one who he can pass to.
- The team's tactics demand the use of aggressive checking.

Passive checking in combination with marking the man and attempting to harass the attack, is used where:

- The checking player is too far away from the puck.
- The opponent with the puck under control is behind the home goal.
- The opponent has the puck under control and has taken up a position facing the center of play.
- The checking player is alone – support from a teammate is missing.
- The team's tactics demand the use of aggressive checking.

The checking player can use the following ice-skating techniques:

- Checking skating forwards.
- Checking or marking the player with the puck by skating backwards.
- Following the opponent dribbling the puck (e.g., backchecking).

### Checking the opponent when skating forwards

Skating quickly up to the opponent who has the puck in a clear area, as well as moving in the correct direction makes for good defensive maneuvers and establishes an important beginning for the whole of the defense. Checking in the correct direction and control of speed are two basic factors, which cause the opponent to move the puck in a particular direction. Checking, done this way, will allow the defender to push the attacker away from the central playing axis towards the boards. At the same time, this will slow down the attack and the opponent can be closed on and marked.

The player doing the checking approaches the opponent skating forwards in a curve so that he pushes him from the central axis in the direction of the boards (see Diagram 65). The correct hold of the stick when doing this is important – the stick is lying on the ice, ready to take on a pass and also to put the opponent with the puck under pressure. If the checker takes the correct direction, he shortens the distance to the player with the puck (see Diagram 66). Body checking or blocking the other player's progress along the boards makes it possible to do a successful tackle (see Diagram 67).

The basic elements of checking by skating forwards are:
- Skate in a curve parallel to the opponent – never at right angles to him.
- Skating between the opponent with the puck and the opponent without the puck (in order to intercept a pass) or stay between the puck and the home goal.
- Force the player with the puck away from the central axis towards the boards.
- Skate in the same direction as the opponent, never in the opposite direction.
- Bit by bit cut down the space the opponent can move in (close marking).
- Match the skating speed of the opponent.
- Keep the blade of the stick on the ice, intercept the opponent's pass and place him under pressure.

**Diagram 65**

**Diagram 66**

**Diagram 67**

### Skating backwards and checking (marking) the opponent dribbling the puck

In this variation, the defender skates backwards facing the opponent. He should be roughly a shoulder width's distance nearer to the central axis than the opponent. This position permits him to mark the center of the ice better and to allow him to react more quickly to the opponent's changes of speed and direction. At the same time the opponent is forced to break out free towards the boards and carry on dribbling there.

The defending player is always between the puck and his own goal with his legs wide apart, knees bent well, upper body and head held up straight. With his eyes he follows the opponent's chest (never the puck). He is holding the stick in one hand in front of him, blade on the ice. The other arm is slightly bent and is held sideways in front of the body. The free arm should provide as broad a warding off position as possible (see Diagram 68).

**Diagram 68**

The basis of successful defense is to rapidly close and check the opponent thus placing him under pressure. This skill should be given the right amount of attention from the beginning. Close marking allows the defender to take the puck away from opponent with his stick without having to have any contact with him. It also allows him to close with the opponent at the right moment and start a tackling action.

The attacking forward always has less room to maneuver in, and the defender must always try to force him away into the desired direction. The next diagram shows various ways of marking.

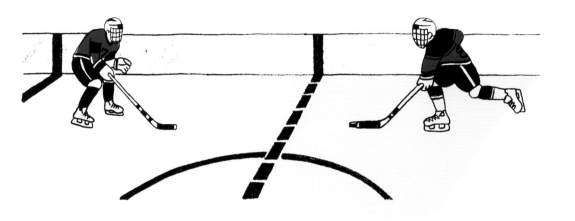

**Diagram 69**

**Chasing the player with the puck (backchecking)**

This term is used where the defender chases the opponent with the puck back into his own defending zone and check him there – i.e., backchecking. Situations also occur where the defender has to skate back to his own half, coming in from behind the opponent in order to backcheck him. Backchecking is particularly used in the neutral zone and where it changes over to the home defending zone and it is necessary to counter an opponent who has penetrated the area. This includes, particularly, the forwards of the defending team.

During backchecking actions, close marking can be also be done on an opponent, who doesn't have the puck. This depends very much on what plans there are for the team's particular defense.

The following ingredients form the basis of the backchecking action:
- When the defender chases the opponent with the puck back into the home half and manages to carry out backchecking actions, he must concentrate on the opponent's body rather than the puck. Otherwise the opposing forward can carry out a dodging movement or break away. When doing the movement it is important to keep the head upright (see Diagram 70).
- Contact with the opponent is limited to skating actions. In no way, may the opponent be illegally checked with the stick (stick-on-body) or by any other form of illegal checking. Closing with the opponent and coming in from the correct

**Diagramm 70**

direction are prerequisites for successful backchecking. When direct contact is made, the player tries to get his shoulder in front of the opponent's. If one comes in too fast, the opponent can make a dodging maneuver by changing direction back behind the defender. It is very bad habit, and illegal in any case, to use the stick-on-body tactic.

- The defender has to close with the opponent with the puck in such a manner so that he is closer to the central axis and his own goal than the attacker.
- If the opponent with the puck manages to penetrate into the shooting zone, the backchecking player must now concentrate on his stick in order to intercept the shot or pass.

## Checking the opponent with the puck along the boards

Besides marking the opponent with the puck in open areas, checking when close to the boards is also important. Clearly, a different kind of technique is demanded here. In practice, this mainly concerns situations behind the goal and along the backboards (for example after backchecking).

Once again, an important factor in this is the optimum timing for closing with the opponent, at the correct angle and at the right speed. The defender must be prepared to react to the changes in the opponent's direction and speed. At the same time, he should be certain that he has the opponent under control (i.e., he doesn't skate at him too fast).

When the player approaches the opponent from behind (for example when backchecking) and from the side, he is facing the boards. He has to match the opponent's skating speed. He holds the stick normally in one hand, the other arm is bent and held slightly sideways in front of the body. The shoulder is over the leading leg and the player is watching the opponent's chest. He stays in between the opponent and the central axis of the ice (or his own goal) (see Diagram 71). By adopting such a position, it leaves little room for the opponent to maneuver in and the defender can control his movements better (starts, stops and change of direction). The defender tries to force the opponent as close to the boards as possible and get himself in a better position for direct contact and taking the puck away. At the right moment, he tries to hook the puck away with his stick or bring it under control or close the opponent down.

**Diagram 71**

After making contact with the body, the player will then try to block the opponent and his stick on the boards and tackle him (see Diagram 72). Either the player takes on the puck himself or a teammate does. When the defender brings pressure onto the opponent's elbow (with the intention of pinning him against the boards), he will have a better chance of getting the puck under control. Care must be taken, however, to distinguish between 'bringing pressure' to bear rather than viciously 'elbowing' the opponent, which is a foul and will attract a penalty. At the same time he will be able to shut the opponent out of the game for a short while and play on himself.

If the opponent manages to pass the puck to one of his teammates, the defender should stay marking the opponent and not follow the puck.

**Diagram 72**

**Checking the opponent with the puck in the defensive zone behind the goal**

This is all about one of the most difficult situations in the defensive zone. For example, in a game 5:5, where the defending team makes a mistake and the opponent manages to get behind the home goal without being marked (checked). The effectiveness of the ensuing defense is not only decided by the technical and tactical experience of the defenders, but also by teamwork, particularly when only one player does the checking. Besides this, it is important that in a situation like this, the goalie also takes part.

When checking the player with the puck in the defensive zone behind the goal there can be two basic situations. In the first case, this is a situation where the opponent with the puck is in a static position behind the goal without being checked. The defender must remain patient. The opponent cannot score a goal from such a position. The basic layout is shown in Diagram 73.

**Diagram 73**

The defender tries to force the opponent into a position where he can make contact with him. That is to say that the player is prepared when the opponent with the puck is closer to him (i.e., to one side of the goal). To do this he uses his stick and carries out various feinting movements. At the right moment, the defender skates in rapidly and makes contact with the opponent (above all against the opponent's stick). He has to try and get between the opponent and the goal. For the defender it is better if he checks the opponent as he is dribbling the puck on his (the opponent's) backhand. When making contact it is important not to lose the tackle and also to make it impossible for the opponent to give a pass. For this the player must concentrate on the player and his stick and not the puck. If the opponent does manage to pass, he continues marking him.

In the second case, this is a situation where the opponent is checked after he has managed to break out free round behind the goal. Where the defender is in contact with the opponent (sometimes, we speak of a distance of half the length of a hockey stick), and is skating at the same or a higher speed, he must keep up with the opponent in order to keep him closely marked. The defender must always keep himself between the puck and his own goal.

In cases where the defender is more than half the length of a hockey stick behind the opponent and has no contact with him, or is skating slower, he checks him behind the goal. The defender takes up a defensive position in front of the goal and then normally a second defenseman undertakes marking and checking the opponent. If the opponent stops behind the goal then the situation as described first comes into play.

### Pinching

In order to understand the complete system of hockey training, mention must be made of a specific variation of checking the opponent with the puck in the attacking zone. However, this skill is practiced first with higher age groups.

The term **pinching** is where a defender checks the opponent with the puck on the boards forward from the blue line. It is a prerequisite that the player is supported by a teammate (see Diagram 74).

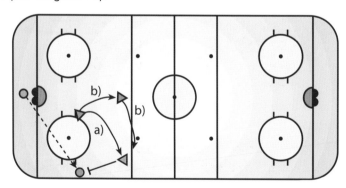

**Diagram 74**

Checking is possible when:

- The defender is supported – either by a defending forward or by a second defenseman (see Diagram 74)
- The checking player is sure that he will win the puck or can mark the attacking forward.

The most suitable moment to carry out the checking action is when the opponent receives a pass on the boards. Success is marked by the ability of the defender to 'read' play correctly – i.e., be able to judge the situation and be able to mark the opponent closely.

## Method

An important prerequisite when training for the checking action is to have the right ice-skating technique. Exercises for it are mainly based on copying the movements of the other player (copy cat games) while skating forwards, backwards and sideways carrying out rapid changes of direction. When checking, the defenseman stays in a defensive posture, in other words he is between the opponent and his own goal or between the player with the puck and another of his teammates. The next diagram shows examples of the exercises.

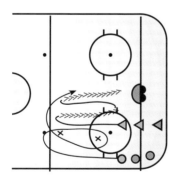 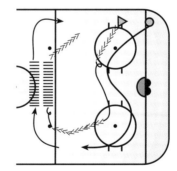

**Diagram 75**

Training for the checking action is best carried out by beginning with skating forwards slowly, at the right angle, with good timing and positioned in clear areas as well as on the boards (exercise examples are in Diagram 76). Here it is important:

- To make contact with the opponent – approaching the opponent in a correct defensive position while skating in a curve. He must be able to control the opponent's movements and be able to react to changes of direction.

- To force the opponent with the puck away from the central axis of the ice onto the boards.
- To skate in the same direction as the opponent (never in the opposite direction).
- Match the opponent's speed.
- To use the stick to hook out the puck or accept a pass and control it, thus placing the opponent under pressure.

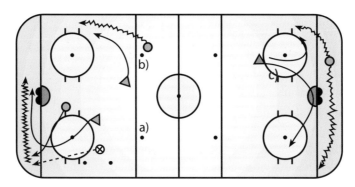

**Diagram 76**

After this, checking training skating backwards is done – posture is legs well apart with knees bent (good position to be able to do quick starts and afford a firm base), hockey stick is in one hand and the player watches the opponent's chest and not the puck. The player is between the opponent with the puck and his own goal. The next diagram shows an exercise for checking of the puck-dribbling opponent with a change from skating forwards to skating backwards. The emphasis is on close marking in such a 1:1 situation.

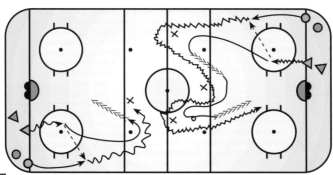

**Diagram 77**

When doing practice in backchecking – back into the own half – while concentrating on ice-skating skills, hooking out and stick checking should be left out. The next diagram shows an example of backchecking in a free space. The exercises should be organized so that the player doing the backchecking is actually able to make contact with the opponent and win the puck off him in a tackle (i.e., it is not a race!).

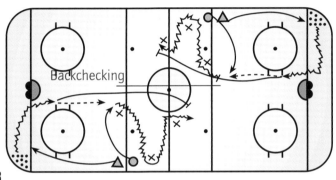

**Diagram 78**

- Checking practice on an opponent dribbling the puck along the boards in all the playing zones on the ice (along the boards, behind the goal crease and in the corners).
- Checking the opponent dribbling the puck in the defense zone behind one's own goal.
- Checking – this activity in defense must be practiced time and time again (first of all using simple preparatory exercises and later using game situations in all parts of the rink).
- When practicing the various defense actions, the trainer must watch that the main aim is to train the defenseman.
- The players change over positions regularly – attacking forwards and defensemen.

## Main mistakes

- Approaching the opponent too obviously – this habit will easily be seen through and allow the opponent to do a feinting maneuver.
- The checking player runs.
- Uncoordinated movements and poor ice-skating techniques.
- Wrong defensive posture.
- The player is too far away from the puck.

## Regaining possession of the puck using the stick

The basic techniques for regaining possession of the puck using the stick were comprehensively covered in the book "Hockey – First Steps for Kids". In order to remind one here what these were, the various different ways are repeated:
- Hooking out the puck.
- Sweep check.
- Hitting the puck away.
- Lifting the stick.
- Pushing the stick away.
- Striking the bottom half of the opponent's stick (against the puck).

In practice, it is important to differentiate between defense with the stick and defense using the body. When tackling, therefore, an optimum combination of the two is what is called for.

## Tackling

Tackling takes place as a continuation of the checking process i.e., getting close to the opponent. Tackling maintains pressure on the opponent with the puck and determines the effectiveness of the defense. Tackling means making body contact with the opponent dribbling the puck.

The main aim for the defender when tackling is to take the puck off the opponent or stop him making a pass. By close marking, it is important to temporarily remove the opponent out of play as he tries to pass the puck or break out free. If the defender is marking properly, then he will be the first player to intervene in play. Tackling is not just about harassing and bundling the dribbling opponent with the body. It is much more the business of actually regaining possession of the puck. Tackling can be done either on the move (in a free area or along the boards) or stationary on the boards.

There are several basic rules for any form of tackling and these should be learned by all young players:
- Always keep the eyes on the opponent's chest and not begin to try to play the puck.
- The necessity to maintain a firm posture – keep the center of gravity of the body low by keeping the legs well apart and the knees bent.

- Keep the head upright – the head should never fall below the line of the shoulders (this is true for the defender as well as the player with the puck).
- The player must always be in the correct position during the tackle – i.e., between the puck and his own goal.
- A player may not unfairly attack the player with the puck from behind when checking, if that player is facing the boards (cross-checking, board-checking).

Training of the basic techniques for tackling should be done step by step. This is so that the defender's skating direction is alternated between forwards and backwards. At the same time, the actual place where the tackle takes place must be considered (along the boards or in a free area). We will now go on to explain a few technical variations.

### Blocking with the body

This variation, where the defending player is skating backwards facing the opponent, is used in tackling along the boards as well as in free areas.

The defender skates in a posture with legs well apart, the stick held in one hand and he is keeping his eyes on the opponent with the puck. The blocking action is done against the opponent's chest in such a way that his free arm is between his own body and that of the opponent. The defender's legs are in the 'T' position. When blocking the opponent the rear leg is tensed so that he can exert greater pressure on the opponent and keep a firm posture (see Diagram 79). The additional work done by the arms is also important. At a suitable moment either the player gains possession of the puck or his teammate does (doubling up).

**Diagram 79**

### Blocking with the shoulders

The technique is often used in situations where the players are face to face and the opponent with the puck tries to penetrate along the boards. The defender holds his stick in both hands and blocks the opponent's chest and stick-carrying arm with his shoulder. It is important to maintain the 'T' position of the legs with knees bent when doing this. The rear leg is also tensed to achieve greater stability in this situation (see Diagram 80).

**Diagram 80**

### Lifting the opponent's stick and blocking him with the shoulder on the boards

The defender is skating forwards along the boards in the same direction as the opponent. He is holding his stick firmly in both hands and he pushes his shoulder a little in front of the opponent. At the moment of contact, he moves the inside bent leg in front of the opponent (the rear leg is tensed firmly – the center of balance of the body is centered over the inside leg). He then places his stick underneath the opponent's stick and lifts it up energetically.

At the same time, he presses the opponent against the boards in a fair manner using his hips and shoulder (called a body check) **Diagram 81** so that the opponent loses the puck and his stick and arms are blocked. The player takes the puck on either with his stick or his skates (see Diagram 81).

## Permissible board-checking

This variation of the defense, done along the boards anywhere round the rink, follows the checking of the puck-dribbling opponent. The attacking forward is shut out of the game for a short moment, during which a teammate is able to regain possession of the puck.

The defender skates forwards along the boards towards the opponent. He is holding the stick wide in both hands just above the ice and approaches the opponent and gets in front of him with his inside shoulder and bent leg. With his arm and shoulder he delivers a permissible push from behind, underneath the opponent's arm and shoulder. As the opponent is turned by this to face the boards, he applies pressure with his leg and hips. He then pushes his own leg, which is in front, between the opponent's legs and presses the opponent against the boards face-on. This blocks, above all, the opponent's stick and arm. Throughout all this he is holding his stick just above the ice and his arms assist in the movements. When maneuvering in these actions, care must be taken not to hold the stick too high illegally (high-sticking) or indeed to carry out any violent elbowing. The player usually takes the puck on with his skate or a teammate helps out (see Diagram 82).

**Diagram 82**

## "Rolling"

This variation of the defense is only done when tackling on the boards. The players are skating in the same direction alongside the boards. After making contact the defender is positioned facing the opponent. Using his shoulder arm, he presses against the upper part of the attacking forward's arm (below the shoulder). The attacker is thus "rolled" against the boards with his chest and loses his stability and control of the puck. This is followed up by quickly blocking his body and stick while the defender takes on the puck with his stick or his skate. In this case, it is also possible for a teammate to take on the puck (doubling up). When doing the action it is important to keep on the move (see Diagram 83). 'Elbowing' and 'high-sticking' are illegal.

**Diagram 83**

The choice of defense variation depends very much on the ice-skating abilities of the defender. The available area in which the tackle takes place (on the boards or in a free area) has also an influence. As already mentioned, the first phase of marking the puck-dribbling opponent is where the checking is done by closing rapidly with him. The body contact and the tackle follow this.

If the player manages to make contact with his body when skating forward in a clear space, he must get his shoulder in front of the opponent as quickly as possible. In this way, the defender is able to get into the correct defensive position (between the opponent and his own goal). When he is not able to regain possession of the puck with one or other of the techniques (see 'Regaining possession of the puck using the stick'), first of all he tries to block the opponent's stick (e.g., by lifting or blocking). The he tries to block the opponent and regain possession of the puck by using his stick or the skate. Use of the arms, within legal rules, to support the movements is very important (see Diagram 84). According to the situation, either the player gets back the puck or his teammate does it for him (doubling up).

**Diagram 84**

When tackling, skating forwards on the boards, the checking player must be able to judge his strength. After making contact, the defender tries to block the opponent's stick and then his body on the boards as quickly as possible, dependent on whether the attacker is facing in towards the center of play on the ice or facing the boards. For this he uses one of the techniques described (blocking with the body, with the shoulder, blocking the stick against the boards etc.). When tackling it is necessary to hold the opponent against the boards. Supporting arm and leg movements also play an important part. If the opponent is being blocked in a position with his back to the boards or front on to the boards, it is advantageous if one places the forward leg between the legs (see Diagram 82). Similarly, placing the stick between the legs will also make it difficult for him to get away. The player is in the 'T' position – heel to heel – with legs wide apart. Both the arms, holding the opponent sideways, support themselves by pressing against the board (Plexiglas). The upper body is leaning on the opponent.

When tackling, skating backwards on the boards as well as in clear, free areas, the defender must always be in the correct defensive position between the puck and his own goal. He is holding the stick in one hand and he keeps his eyes on the opponent's chest – not the puck. Skating with legs well apart and knees bent, he has a good stable posture and can do starts and change direction quickly. When tackling, it is better to have the weight of the body centered over the leg that is farthest away from the direction of the tackle. As already described in checking, the defender should be a shoulder width nearer the central axis than his opponent (when tackling in free areas). The defender makes contact with his shoulder first of all and only then does he use his arms, the stick and the body. Again, legal use of the arms in support of the block is important. After blocking, the defender takes the puck on himself (with his stick or skate) or he leaves it for his teammate. The next diagram shows how the player approaches the opponent with the puck in a clear area and how he blocks him.

**Diagram 85**

## Body play – the body check

The most complicated of all the defense techniques using the body is trained as a last item for children in the higher classes. In order to maintain the hockey training system, however, the basic technique of the body check will be covered at this juncture (so that the variations in marking the player with the puck are referred to in sequence).

One of the main things here is to differentiate between the body check and the tackling action. Body checking is understood as making the opponent stop, blocking him with a hard movement of the body (from the shoulders down to the hips). In practice, however, the body check is done mainly with the hips, bottom and the shoulders. Body checking only with the shoulders is, in practice, difficult to do and actually belongs to the action in tackling of blocking with the shoulder. This variation is described elsewhere. Therefore, here, we will only cover the body check with the hips (bottom).

It concerns an effective attack on the opponent with the puck in a free area or on the boards. Its psychological effect is particularly influential. Where a defender is able to successfully carry out several body checks within the first few minutes of a game, generally speaking, this will have a negative effect on the opponent. A good moment for doing a body check is when the opponent is following his puck (taking on a pass, doing a feinting maneuver), or when he is trying to play round another defender or dodge him. In order for the movement to be effective, correct posture, the correct technique and the optimum preparation for the clash of bodies are all important.

This defensive variation, using the body, is done in two phases. In the first phase, the player must get near to the opponent. So that the body check is successful, this phase (change of direction) has to be done quickly and with an element of surprise. The defender comes into contact with the opponent, either by skating backwards or diagonally forwards.

At the moment of the body check – clashing with the hips – the defender is skating backwards and at right angles to the direction taken by the opponent. He achieves a firm base by having legs well apart and knees bent with the stick in one hand. By executing a sideways and upward movement of the pelvis at the right moment, he clashes with the opponent. At that moment, the leg farthest away from the opponent is tensed and the center of gravity of the body is lifted up a little.

## The body check on the boards

This variation of body play is often used. The defender, skating backwards, makes a defensive feinting movement in a 1:1 situation and forces the opponent to skate free away down the boards. If the opponent with the puck then actually does penetrate along the boards, the defender turns himself round (the center of gravity of the body is lowered) and clashes against the opponent with his hip or pelvis. As the strike goes in, the leg farthest away from the opponent is tensed firmly (see Diagram 86).

**Diagram 86**

## The body check in a free area

The technique used is similar to the previous one above, but the execution is more strenuous than the body check on the boards. The opponent has more space available to get away as the defender comes in with a right-angled skating approach. It is therefore important that the turn is done at the very last moment as he skates in at top speed (see Diagram 87).

**Diagram 87**

**Game situation 1:1 (as seen from the defender's point of view)**

Everything that has been written about 1:1 situations from an attacker's point of view, is also valid for the defense. Once again, it must be recalled that any solution for a 1:1 situation (in a proper game as well as in training) is influenced, amongst other things, by three main characteristics:

■ By the area in which the situation takes place.
■ By the individual technical and tactical skills of the defending player.
■ By the individual technical and tactical skills of the attacking forward.

Defense in tight areas in all the playing zones and areas of the ice rink forms the basis of defense play for the whole team. When the individual players are able to master the various defense actions well, this gives a good basis for training defense combinations and systems.

Free areas on the whole of the ice, areas along the boards, playing down the central axis of the ice, the shooting area, defense on the blue attack and defense lines, penetration by the opponent into the defense zone down the center and along the boards, defense behind the home goal, defense in situations where the opponent comes into the defense zone from the corner etc., are all practical examples of areas suitable for training and using exercise variations. Only by practicing these situations will the young player gain sufficient confidence, which he can use later with his own experience and begin to perfect his skill at improvising.

The young players should not begin to learn game combinations and game systems until they can completely master ice-skating and the individual playing skills.

### Methods in tackling

■ For training in tackling, the basics of good ice-skating are absolutely essential.
■ Various copy cat and reaction exercises, with changes of direction incorporated, are used as preparatory work for this skill (examples are shown in Diagram 88).
■ In training, note must be made of the different ice-skating skills required for checking and marking (see Diagram 89).

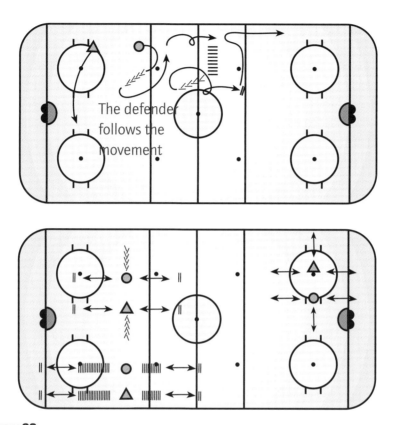

The defender follows the movement

**Diagram 88**

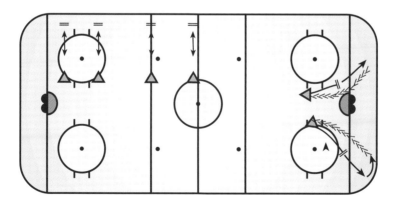

**Diagram 89**

- When training in pairs, the children should be roughly matched in size and weight.
- When training it should be made very clear whether the exercises are aimed at attack or defense – above all, in the first phase, the playing actions should be simplified.
- Simple exercises should be carried out with the emphasis on adopting the correct defensive posture relative to the opponent with the puck and the own goal (so-called 'on the defensive side') (see Diagram 90).

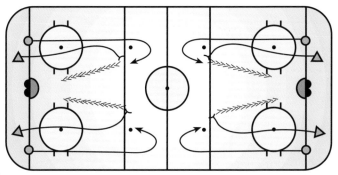

**Diagram 90**

- The next training step provides exercises for the marking of the puck-dribbling player, seen from a viewpoint of how busy the marking area is (area and man marking relative to the distance from the own goal). The next diagram shows an exercise of close marking after a movement of the puck-dribbling player in the direction of goal.

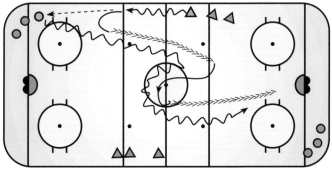

**Diagram 91**

■ Training exercises are divided into those to practice the defender's ice-skating skills and those to do with marking in the various areas of the ice (see Diagram 92 a, b, c & d).

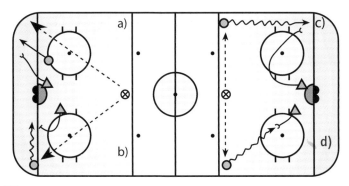

**Diagram 92**

■ In all the exercises, the players regularly changeover playing as defenders and attackers.

■ The trainer explains the individual defense variations in steps (better still using video or a demonstration by a member of the first team).

■ Training begins off the ice (little games etc.).

■ Tackling is explained and demonstrated on the ice.

■ Exercises are done standing still, without an opponent and in the direction of the boards.

■ Exercises with an opponent (game forms – pressing etc.).

■ Exercises in pairs done slowly on the move – in free areas and along the boards (frequent changeovers).

■ Practice close marking in the free areas and along the boards.

■ Special game exercises with the emphasis on tackling in various playing areas – same situation as in tackling 1:1 seen from the viewpoint of the attacker.

■ Checking and tackling when skating forwards and backwards, and above all, using a combination of the two.

■ Playing in a confined space with the emphasis on tackling.

■ Using the body and the body check should not be done as a main theme in a training session aimed at emphasizing marking the puck-dribbling opponent.

■ Training for these defensive actions should be seen more as complementing exercises in the training session for the younger age-group classes.

- The players should be taught the body check after they have managed to master all of the other tackling variations.
- First of all, training is carried slowly without an opponent and with the aim of skating an accurate and rapid curve (change of direction), and stressing the lowering of the center of gravity of the body.
- The next step is to train in pairs, moving slowly.
- The exercises are carried out both skating backwards and diagonally forwards.
- After mastering the skills, training is conducted in game forms – when doing so, the activities must be constructed to avoid the risk of injury to the attacking forwards.

## Main mistakes

- The movements are done at right angles to the opponent with the puck.
- The players concentrate too much on the technique of tackling and do not register the opponent's changes of direction.
- The defender is too upright when he tackles – wrong posture.
- The player watches the puck rather than the opponent.
- Contact is made too late.
- The action is begun too far away from or too near to the opponent.
- During the tackle, the player fails to attempt to gain the puck.
- The hockey stick is held too high – possible illegal attack or injury of the opponent.
- The player carries out the tackle, but is afraid of being hit by the opponent.
- The player leans over forward when tackling – risk of injury.

### General basic rules for tackling training with the aspect of avoiding injuries

Tackling (either in defense or in the attack) features a clashing of the players' bodies or against the boards. Therefore, the young players have to learn not only the correct technique, but also how to act so that they do not injure themselves or their opponent. The player must always avoid being injured, irrespective of whether they are doing the checking or are being checked themselves. Although, in the youngest age groups, direct body contact is not allowed, very often contact between players and, above all, against the boards does occur.

The following rules should serve to help all players avoid injuries. These are valid for both the checking player and the one being checked.

- The rule is: "Never check the opponent with the puck illegally from behind" – cross-checking with the stick, board-checking etc.
- Use good equipment.
- Hold the head up well (when making contact with the boards, the head must not get lower than the level of the shoulders).
- Always watch what the opponent is doing.
- Stay on the move, mainly when in the neighborhood of the boards. When on the move the player can react better to the body check.
- Maintain a stable posture with a lowered center of gravity of the body (knees bent and legs shoulder width apart).
- If there is a danger of colliding with the head against the boards, then the player has to bring his arms forward immediately. At the same time he tries to turn so that he collides with the boards sideways.
- When the player is sideways on to the boards, he holds his head upright and lowers the center of gravity of his body (legs apart sideways, knees bent). He tries to cushion the collision with the boards with the largest area of his body – with the arms, hips and shoulders, never only with the shoulders or the head (see Diagram 93). The collision is cushioned with the whole arm nearest to the boards (not only with the elbow).

**Correct**                                                           **Wrong**

**Diagram 93**

Where the player finds himself facing the boards, he should absorb the collision with the largest area of his body. The most important thing is to keep the head upright. It should never be held leaning forward and become the first thing to collide with the boards. The player can absorb the collision using his arms and the stick, which he lifts up (see Diagram 94). Keeping the legs parallel to the boards in a correct posture also plays an important role. If the player, however, collides with the boards with his skates at right angles to them, when he makes contact he will lose his balance straight away.

**Diagram 94**

## Practical tips for the trainer

- Irrespective of whether it is in training or a game, when tackling, any form of violent play (long run-up before actually making contact, overaggressive play etc.,) must be categorically forbidden.

- The stick must always be kept down.

- When playing the game, cries of encouragement such as "Dig him in the body!"; "Go on, show him!" should also not be allowed.

- For children, the action of gaining back the puck should always be preferred to carrying out a tackle.

- In case of injury occurring during a tackle (either to the home player or the opponent) this must never be played down and ignored. The health of the children is always more important than success.

- If the opponent is playing too hard and violently, the trainer should point out to his colleagues on the other team that such play is not suitable for 9-10 year-olds. He should also point this out to his own team of course.

- The trainer spurs his own players on to be courageous – here he is furthering their self-confidence (confidence in their own skills).

## 7.2 Marking the Player without the Puck

Marking a player, who doesn't have the puck, is a further individual defensive action. Which type of marking of the player without the puck that is to be used, is determined by the density of the defense system employed by the whole team. In simpler words – it is all about an action, which prevents the opponents from breaking out free and taking on a pass. Marking the player without the puck when withdrawing back down the ice, above all in the neutral zone, is known as backchecking the opponent without the puck. This activity is not well liked. Despite this, it should be paid a great deal of attention in training and in competition. Bad habits, which the young players develop and become the norm, have a negative affect on performance later on.

The effectiveness of marking the opponent without the puck is dependent mainly on the various ways used and on the closeness of the marking. A prerequisite for the correct marking of the opponent without the puck is for the defender to be in the correct position. He should always be on the so-called inside of the defense (see Diagram 95), with the aim of getting immediately in front of the opponent.

**Diagram 95**

This position allows the defender to get in between the opponent and his own goal (see Diagram 96) or between the opponent and the puck (see Diagram 97) (two marking variations).

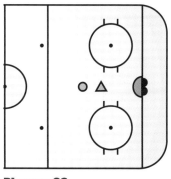

**Diagram 96**

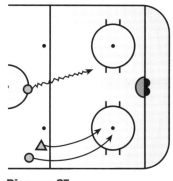

**Diagram 97**

The choice of one of the suitable variations is, above all, dependent on:
- The game situation.
- The space available (playing zone).
- The defender's skating style (skating backwards, forwards), as well as...
- The defense strategy.

The defender can mark the opponent without the puck by skating either forwards or backwards. When marking by skating forwards in the neutral playing zone this is called backchecking – see Diagram 98.

**Diagram 98**

There are certain principles employed when backchecking the player without the puck, just as there are when he has the puck. It is necessary to mention some of them here:
- When chasing, pick the head up and watch the opponent, the puck and the other players.
- Close with the opponent only use skating movements (don't hook in or use the stick in any other way).
- The defender must get into the correct defensive position (on the "inside of the defense") and be either between the opponent and the puck or between the opponent and his own goal.
- There is a rule, which says that the nearer one is to the home goal, the closer the opponent without the puck has to be marked.
- If the opponent manages to get into the shooting zone, from where he could threaten the goal after receiving a pass, the backchecker should concentrate, above all, on the opponent's stick.

When marking the opponent while skating backwards, the defender has to get in between the opponent and his own goal. However, this variation demands good agility on the ice, above all when changing over from skating backwards to sideways and then forwards. According to the game situation and play area, the trainer must watch that sufficient marking is being carried out. Once upon a time, this type of marking was the duty of the defenders. In modern hockey the differences between positions played in defense are not important any more. From the viewpoint of the whole of the defense strategy, the thing that matters is the space where the player is at any one time. The next diagram shows close marking in a situation where the defender is skating backwards.

**Diagram 99**

As soon as the young players have learned the basics of marking when skating forwards and backwards, they can then do combinations of them both together. The next parameter, on which marking of the opponent is measured, is its density. There is, of course, man marking and area marking.

Man marking means that the defender is in contact with the attacking forward. This variation can be done using the body, the arm or the stick. All attacking forwards must be marked closely when they are in front of the goal or in the shooting zone. For this variation, it is also important that the close marking includes closely blocking the opponent's stick and not using man marking. The basic prerequisites for defending successfully in such a situation is to have the optimum defense posture, a firm base and determination. The player doing the marking watches not only "his" opponent, but also the player with the puck and the other players.

When conducting area marking, the players are not in contact with each other. It is essential to maintain a distance that enables the player to changeover to man marking at any moment in play.

In modern top-class hockey, man marking is combined with zone defense. The young players must learn the general rule that in their own half of the ice, they have to mark the opponent as closely as possible (where the game situation allows this). Close marking of the opponent is also recommended for players whose ice-skating skills are not so good. After mastering the technical basics and the principles of marking, the defense system using direct defense and zone defense is explained and practiced.

A firm element of marking practice are exercises, which have the emphasis on marking the player, who is passing the puck. The attention of most players is on the opponent with the puck. The attacking forward, who passes the puck, is usually skating in a free space, which is very dangerous for the defending team. This is irrespective of whether the situation is during the attack build-up, its development or its conclusion. The young players must practice this action (marking the opponent, who passes the puck on). In different ice hockey nations, this is sometimes neglected in comparison to others. The next diagram shows an example of an exercise.

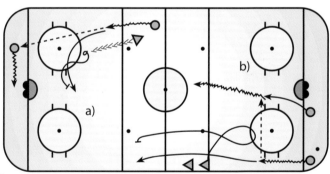

**Diagram 100**

After mastering the marking variations, skating forwards and backwards, mentioned above, the older players now train marking the players without the puck and who skate behind the player with the puck in formation. This concerns game situations in the neutral zone as well as the transition into the defending zone, and above all, for situations where the defense zone has been penetrated. The defender takes up a position each time between the opponent and the goal. The defender is on the move so that he can closely mark the opponent. It is imperative that the defender does not become too static and dodge the opponent by skating backwards ("wait for the opponent"). The defender tries to push the opponent away from the central axis of play by using legal movements. An example of this is shown in the next diagram.

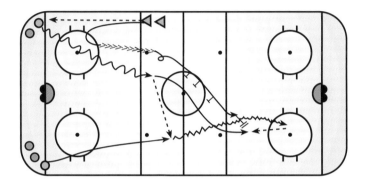

**Diagram 101**

Connected with marking the second player, complementary exercises in marking the player without the puck, who comes up to join in (the "second attack wave"). In general, both the player with the puck as well as the player in the second attack wave have to be watched carefully. Marking is mostly done as one skates backwards employing frequent sideways cross-overs. The defending players are always on the move and they should not just sit and wait for the opponents (see Diagram 102).

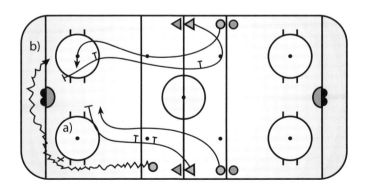

**Diagram 102**

## Methods

- Two (three) players are moving slowly. The attacking player changes his direction and the defending players "watch out for him". On a signal all skate faster (see Diagram 103).

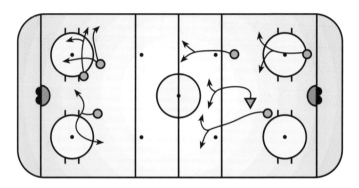

**Diagram 103**

- The exercise with the "watch out" is done skating forwards, backwards and in a combination of both of them.

- Two (three) players; the attacking player tries to breakaway into a free area, but the defender marks him closely. The trainer passes the puck into play (see Diagram 104).

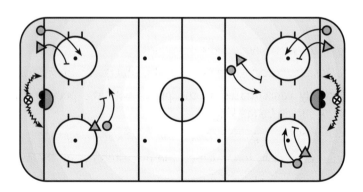

**Diagram 104**

- When marking, the defender skates forwards and backwards.
- Exercises with backchecking (see Diagram 105).

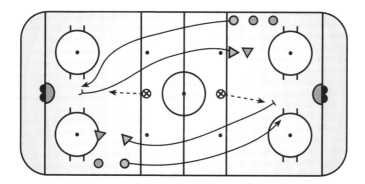

**Diagram 105**

- Short game play with individual defense.
- Exercises in a confined space using man marking and area marking.

## Rules for the player

- Marking the player without the puck is not considered to be interference.
- When marking, the defender skates at the same speed as the opponent.
- The defender is always on the "inside of the defense".
- A player without the puck, who is marked properly cannot be active in play any more (he is shut out of play).

## Main mistakes

- The defender is too far away from the opponent
- The defender loses contact (visible or physical contact) with the attacking player.
- The defender only concentrates on the player with the puck and not on the attacker that he should be marking.
- Marking of the stick is not properly carried out in the shooting zone.
- The defender concentrates too much on the puck and not on the movements of the player that he should be marking.

## 7.3   Area Marking

This term is understood as marking an area (area marking) as well as marking a player in an area where he actually is or where he is heading for.

Marking a player in an area is, in principle, an action that is connected with the marking of a player without the puck.

Area marking is a defense action that is carried out when the game arrives at a situation where the attacking forwards are a 'man up' over the defenders (man advantage). This is usually in situations of proportions of 2:1; 3:1 and 3:2 and where the defenders are in an optimum position to defend the area and try to impede the attackers. The situation is dangerous when the defender watches the puck and turns his back on the opponent. The defender's duty is not only to closely mark the opponent in the area, but also to mark the area on the other side of the puck and control this (see Diagram 106).

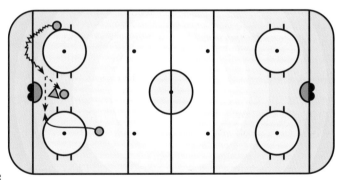

**Diagram 106**

## Methods

For this activity, the choice of solution demands certain tactical experience from the defender. For this age group, the players are only introduced to the basics of the playing actions. Only later, should the different tactical variations be explained and practiced, and then, as they come up in play.

- Area defense in a situation 2:1 is practiced at slow speed (see Diagram 107).

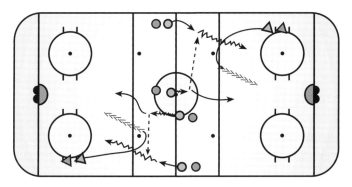

**Diagram 107**

- Practice exercise 2:1 with area marking.
- Slowly practice area marking in a situation 3:1.
- Practice exercise with area marking 3:1.
- Practice exercise 2:1; 3:1 with defense against a player already in the area.
- For older age groups practice exercises with 3:2.

## Rules for the player

- Dodging in the neighborhood of the central axis and trying to push the opponent into a less favorable position in the direction of the boards.
- Placing the stick onto the ice in front of the player, in order to be able to intercept a pass.
- Working in cooperation with the goalie in front of the goal.
- Slowing down the action so that the teammates can get back into play (equal numbers).
- Keeping as close a distance to the attacking forward and when possible carry out a defensive action.

## Main mistakes

- Starting the defensive action too soon – checking a single player.
- Concentrating too much on a single player.
- The defensive action fails (even in the immediate vicinity of the goal).
- After starting the defensive action, the player in an area is not marked.

## 7.4 Blocking and Stopping Shots

Blocking and stopping shots is mainly done in the defending zone with the aim of increasing the effectiveness of the defense. The ability to block or stop a shot or only alter its direction at the right moment, is a firm element of a defender's job. This ability is very valuable against shots done by the defenders from the blue attack line and this even in a game 5:5 as well as in outnumbered situations. From a tactical viewpoint, the blocking technique is used against particularly good shooting opponents.

Blocking and stopping shots with the puck are defined as individual defense play actions where the player tries to change the flight of the puck away from the goal.

In practice, there are four basic variations of blocking and stopping puck shots used:
- While standing.
- Kneeling down on one or both knees.
- By using the sliding prone position.
- With the stick.

### Blocking the shot while standing

This variation is used against shots from different distances. The player blocking stands facing the opponent and his stance is in a lowered center of gravity of the body with legs shoulder width apart. He is holding the stick sideways in one hand to the side of his body or in front of the body like the goalie. The free arm is held down by the side of the body and the palm of the hand is facing forwards (in case he can use it to catch the puck). Such a posture is optimum, not only to block shots, but also it gives him the opportunity to changeover into a defensive posture in case the opponent decides to do a feint instead of shooting.

### Blocking the shot, kneeling down on one or both knees

In this variation, it is important that the defender is not too far away from the puck-dribbling opponent and that he is in a right-angled position facing him. There is a danger of injury otherwise.

When kneeling on one knee, the defender is always able to get back quickly into the basic standing position. The stick is held by its pommel end in one hand, sideways from the body and just over or on the ice. The trunk is upright and the free arm is held down by the side of the body with the palm of the hand facing forwards. Placing the skate of the bent knee in an optimum position gives him the possibility to react quickly in case the opponent only fakes a shot (see Diagram 108).

**Diagram 108**

The second variation of blocking and stopping the shot is where the player kneels down on both knees. This way the high shot and the flat shot can both be stopped. This version is often used from a backwards skating position when the defender dodges back from the opponent. At the moment that the opponent is about to shoot, the defender rapidly drops down on both knees holding the stick sideways in one hand and with the free arm down by the side of his body with the palm facing forwards. In this variation, the defender will also be quite close to the attacking shooter (danger of injury).

**Blocking the shot using the sliding prone position**

The defender drops down into a sliding prone position (just like the goalie does). To do this he lies down in a sideways position on the ice with his legs, one on top of the other. The stick is held in one hand by the pommel and the arm holding it is laid down along the ice. The free arm is held down the side of the body with the palm facing forwards (see Diagram 109). The player should fall down and make a right angle with his legs to the direction of the blade of the opponent's stick (with his head furthest away from the shooting player where possible. Blocking the shot using the sliding prone position makes for a large area to be covered efficiently. The shot can also be blocked and stopped, even if the player is not at right angles to the opponent when he shoots.

**Diagram 109**

**Blocking the shot with the stick**

The defender places the blade of his stick in front of the puck just at the moment when the shot is made. This variation is used in situations when the defender has no contact with the opponent. Blocking shots can be carried out at any distance desired from the shooting player. The defender has to take note of the position of the blade of his stick (looking to make the optimum angle). When the puck shoots or bounces upwards as it hits the blade, there is a danger of injury. Similarly, an uncontrolled block of a shot can also endanger the goalie.

## Methods

- A prerequisite for training in this individual defense tactic is a good, complete set of hockey equipment. There is a danger of injury involved and the young players are afraid of being hit by the puck.
- Correctly mastering each of the techniques increases the effectiveness of play and the player's interest in the game.
- All variations of the blocking technique are similar when it comes to practicing them.
- First of all, the basic movements are practiced without the puck.
- Then, practice against a gently hit puck (see Diagram 110).

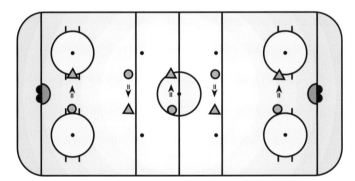

**Diagram 110**

- Block the puck coming in.
- Now block a puck coming in faster – this is done carefully and first of all, with the older classes.

**Rules for the player**

- When kneeling down, either on one or both knees, the stick is always to the side of the body and the defender must not be too far away from the player making the shot.
- When doing the sliding prone block, the player must fall down in the direction towards the opponent's blade – the head is pointing in the other direction.
- Don't turn the head away and always keep an eye on the puck.

## Main mistakes

- Turning sideways or turning the back on the puck.
- When doing the sliding prone block, the head is pointing towards the puck.
- Shying away from the puck – being afraid of it.
- Inadvertently deflecting the puck in the immediate vicinity of the home goal.

# 8 Coordination Ability

**T**his chapter is a summary and a continuation of the training for perfecting the individual playing actions. Coordination exercises belong to the most effective methods of developing individual playing actions and improve the whole team's cooperation. These exercises are a firm part in the training process for the 9-10 year-olds. The reason for this is the optimum ability of the central nervous system to pick up the motor learning at this age. Another reason is the long period of time required for learning these exercises.

### Coordination exercises and biological development

Just as it is with other movement abilities, the ability to coordinate is connected with the biological and physical development of the child. In comparison with other abilities, these are based on single forms of the functioning of the central nervous system, which, in principle, are teachable at any age. (This is, however, not always effective). A summary of the knowledge to date regarding motor development shows that the human organism at an age of about 10 years old is particularly amenable to the development of the coordination ability (i.e., to the individual parts of the body). Training should be kept general. For the exercises, these should include exercises for the individual parts of the body as well as the whole body (both sides of the body, movements forwards, backwards etc.).

### Principles for the preparation of coordination exercises

There are no standard training parameters that characterize weight loading in the coordination exercises. The high demands on the central nervous system and on the execution of movements lead to practical principles and recommendations. They are also valid for the development of the ability to be agile:
- Coordination exercises with increasing difficulty.
- Several actions being done at any one time.
- Activities that have already been mastered should be carried out in a different form.
- Doing exercises under pressure.
- Exercises with additional information – what purpose the exercise performs.
- Exercises carried out after previous exertion.

### Breaking down the coordination exercises into parts

The coordination exercises are broken down into individual and team exercises. Individual exercises are designed to perfect personal playing actions.

Team exercises are aimed at furthering cooperation amongst the players. These team skills, however, are taught to older players and therefore will not be covered here.

### Individual coordination exercises

As already indicated, the individual coordination exercises serve to perfect the individual playing actions that have already been learned. They should be particularly so constructed exactly for this age group. Several exercises are described in the following:

- Puck handling.
- Dribbling with elements of agility thrown in (kneeling on one knee, sitting down, when jumping, when turning round).
- Dribbling the puck in a tight area (in one of the playing zones).
- Dribbling doing turns (standing, kneeling, on one leg).
- Dribbling when skating on one leg (curves round on the inside and the outside edges of the skate, changing edges when skating in a snaking form).
- Dribbling the puck through a slalom (of small cones).
- Doing a slalom course with tests of agility (jumping over things, turns, ducking under obstacles, dodging).
- Changing direction at a signal when puck handling.
- Different, unusual ways of doing puck handling (holding the stick differently, several pucks at the same time, using the stick and the skate at the same time etc.).
- Passing.
- Passing in a circle (one player in the middle tries to intercept the pass).
- Playing passing over hurdles.
- Passing using a tennis ball.
- Passing in different directions, striking the puck only once each time.
- Doing shots at goal.
- Repeated shots from a standing position and on the move.
- Doing rapid shooting with several pucks.
- Doing shots without any preparation in various different goal areas.

- Shooting after doing an agility test.
- Doing shots between and when going over hurdles.
- Exercises combining playing skills.
- Combinations of passes, agility exercises (turns, kneeling on one knee, kneeling on both knees, jumps) and then doing a shot.
- Repeated passes followed by a shot at goal.
- Various different types of shot according to the game situation.
- Shots with additional information as to the aim of the exercise.
- Play exercises.
- Doing a large number of agility exercises together.
- Doing several deliberate changes of play according to the game situation.

## Training suggestions

- When doing coordination exercises, the players should be placed in extreme game situations.
- Coordination exercises have their own philosophy, about which the trainer should give an explanation for the players to note.
- The exercises cross several boundaries i.e., what the player can still achieve and what he cannot.
- The exercises are used regularly and over a long period of time.
- Doing coordination exercises should be begun already when the children are still young.
- Before doing the exercises, the theory of them should be explained. The children should have learned the necessary skills already off the ice.
- It is not necessary that all of the players be able to master the exercises from the beginning.

# 9
# The Face-off
# (A Particular Game Action)

The whole of this chapter, devoted to the face-off, is really outside the realms of this book. Nevertheless, we are going to include a description of the basic technique of facing off. Using the framework of the standard, methodical layout, at the end of the chapter we will make some suggestions for suitable techniques for this age group (9-10 year-olds).

In keeping with the system in ice hockey, the face-off is a particular game action, because the activity cannot be determined as a defensive or an attack movement before it is carried out. It is only the result of the face-off that shows which team has won the puck.

Publications that deal with this problem skim over the points all too quickly. They mainly concentrate on the tactics of the face-off (and then only over the tactical variations following the successful gaining of the puck). The correct technique is then, as a result, often underestimated. Besides this, the rapid, unbroken development of play, brought about by the changes in the rules, makes some of the previously described techniques are, in principle, no longer allowable. In this book, we will therefore cover the face-off under various aspects, so that the system and the technique described will be in accordance with the modern game and the international rules.

The face-off, as an action with which play is begun, is one of the most specific actions in ice hockey. The action is carried out in a standardized manner with the puck being dropped-in between two players at the beginning of each of the thirds of play and after each break in play. The positions of the players are laid down in the rules. This type of play action, therefore, has to be seen in this light regarding techniques and tactics.

According to the latest statistics, there are about 60-90 face-offs during the course of any one competitive game. These statistics back up the fact that a player in a game can be anywhere up to 70% effective in the face-off.

Seen from a physiological point of view, the action concerns a very short, acyclic strain with high demands on the coordination of the muscular and nervous systems.

The respiratory and circulatory systems are only minimally in demand. The demand for energy is drawn from the biological reserves from the ATP-CP area and is seen as being combined mainly with the action between the two players following the face-off, and which last no longer than 3 seconds.

In the drop-in, the length of time taken to react and the length of the action itself (the time taken to execute the movement) are the deciding factors. The length of time it takes to react depends on the speed of reaction and the length of action itself is dependent on the strength ability and technique. Playing the puck forward is a shorter movement than playing it rearwards. Therefore, this variation is quicker.

Regarding the hold taken on the hockey stick (dependent on the length of the action itself), the following grip has proved to be the one that produces the quicker timings: The upper hand doesn't take hold just below the pommel (as when playing normally), rather it holds it about 30 cms lower. The lower hand adjusts itself accordingly and takes hold about 20 cms further down.

From all this we can see that the face-off is influenced by speed and strength (besides the activity of the central nervous system).

The face-off is influenced, like other game situations, by certain factors. In this case, these constitute four main ones – technique, tactics, fitness and the mind. In this book here, we only cover the aspect of the technique.

## 9.1 Carrying out the Face-off

So that the whole system makes sense and is clear, the technique and the tactics of the face-off will be described separately. However, in practice there are no firm boundaries between the two areas, because they each have an influence on each other.

With the term 'technique of the face-off' we understand this to be a particular way of gaining possession of the puck. The choice of the variation determines the tactics in a specific game situation.

For training and perfecting the face-off, the following system is used:

## Technique of the face-off

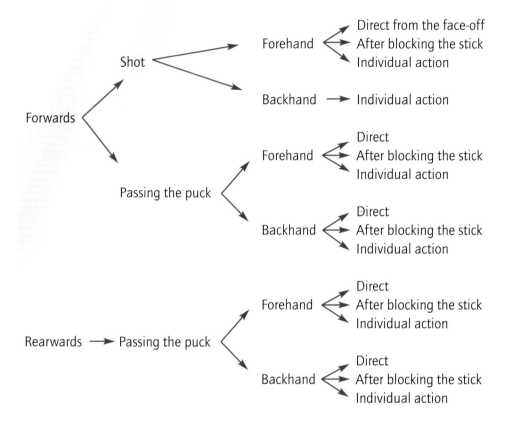

## Tactics in the face-off

Several basic tactics are distinguished from each other, based on the number of players taking part in the game situation.

■ Individual tactical solution

**Individual action forwards** – this variation is only seldom chosen (1-2 times per game). It is more about exploiting the moment of surprise in the attacking zone. The players usually adapt their formation in such a way that its use is spoiled for the opponent. The effectiveness of this variation is very low, and therefore it is only used where the loss of the puck will not play a decisive role.

**Shot direct from the face-off** – the effectiveness of this method is rather low. As a result, its use is sporadic (mainly shortly before the end of play). The player, who is going to carry out this technique, must not give away his intention by the stance he adopts when taking the face-off.

**Lying down on the puck** – this is a spoiling tactic, which is used first of all when the original intention fails and the player chooses to take the disadvantage of a break in play rather than simply lose the puck.

**Forced change-round of players** – similarly, this is also a spoiling tactic with the aim of forcing a change of players. Normally, when the player provokes the other by reacting prematurely – stick against stick or hitting the opponent's legs – the initiator of the action is the one who is penalized. When there is a face-off specialist on the ice, this variation is used in particularly important playing phases.

**Referee causes a puck to bounce up** – this is a situation where the puck bounces away from the players without them having touched it. In practice it can be seen that, if neither player hits the puck it bounces in the direction of the player, who is standing more facing the referee. If the referee is standing to the right of the center forward, the puck tends to bounce away to the left. The players must watch out for this and not allow the opponent to get to the puck faster.

**Illegal contact with the puck before it hits the ice** – the rules do not permit this variation and it depends on the referee and how he judges it. If he blows up for illegal play, this is when the players change round for the face-off. Because of this, this variation is often used. This concerns playing forwards as well as sideways and rearwards.

- **Tactical team solution**

In the face-off, tactics are influenced by further factors. The most important of these are:
- Area and zone where the face-off takes place.
- The number of players (equal situations 5:5, 4:4; man advantage 5:4, 5:3, 4:3; and short-handed 4:5 etc.).
- Score and phase of the game (leading, tied score, end of the period or of the game etc.).
- How good the opponent is in the face-off (his good points, weaknesses, how he holds the blade of the stick on the face-off spot, how he holds his stick etc.). This factor will have an influence on the choice of the technique to counter it and the individual tactic.

## 9.2   Timing – Length of Action

The choice of individual face-off technique (the tactics) is particularly influenced by this factor. The length of action is deliberately dealt with separately so that three face-off variations with different lengths of action can be described.

**Direct pass of the puck**

This variation is one of the quickest possibilities and relies on rapid reaction and exact execution of the technique. The player concentrates on the puck in the referee's hand and must have a good feeling for an accurate pass in the right direction. High speed in the action that follows is of great advantage. Low effectiveness and lack of precision are disadvantageous. A blocking action by the opponent's stick is relatively effective in hindering the stroke. The effectiveness is also lowered if the puck is not hit squarely, or in cases where the puck bounces after the referee drops it in (see Diagram 111).

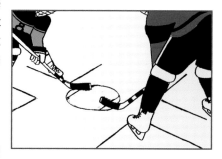

**Diagram 111**

**Clashing sticks with a follow-up pass**

In most cases this is to do with clashing with the opponent's stick and with a follow-up pass. The longer time it takes to execute this action, however, makes it possible for the opponent to counter the movement. This is one of the disadvantages of this technique. The advantages are its high precision and the possibility of using this variation in practically all the playing zones and in any situation (see Diagram 112).

**Diagram 112**

### Players clashing in the face-off

This is the variation, which takes the longest time to do. The rules do not allow this variation to be done deliberately. The reason for this is that the player ends mainly in blocking the opponent and passing the puck out with the leg or with the aid of a teammate (or catching it in the air), which are not allowed by the rules. Such clashes, however, do occur in spite of this, because some referees are more tolerant and also because of the fact that it is difficult to judge when and which players touched the puck.

It is therefore necessary to go well into describing the tactical variations. The disadvantages of this variation are that surprise is lost and because of the great demands placed on the steadiness of the players can also be of use. Some variations are used as spoiling techniques aimed at disrupting the build-up of the opponent's attack.

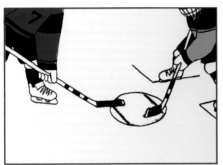

The player is in a normal position with the stick held by the lower hand gripping. He centers his body weight more on the tips of the skates. The player should not support himself by leaning on his stick on the ice (see Diagram 113 the player on the left).

**Diagram 113**

After the puck has been dropped in, the left-handed player pushes his left leg against the opponent and tries to prevent the puck being passed (stick block or lifting the stick) (see Diagram 114).

**Diagram 114**

Turning his body, he prevents the opponent getting at the puck. As he does this, he turns his back on the opponent. He then plays the puck, either with his stick or his leg. At that moment he can chose any of the variations of continuing play (taking a shot, passing or another individual action) (see Diagram 115).

**Diagram 115**

Before the basic techniques of the face-off can be described, some of the terms used must be explained.

■ A left-handed player (holding the stick to the left) is one who holds the stick with his left hand nearer to the blade than the other.

■ A right-handed player (holding the stick to the right) is one who holds the stick with his right hand lower than the left hand.

■ The over grip – the player holds the stick with the lower hand grasping over the stick so that the back of the hand is facing upwards (not downwards like in play) (see Diagram 116).

■ The under grip – the player holds the stick as he would do when playing (see Diagram 116).

**Diagram 116:**
**The player on the left is holding the stick with an over grip and the player on the right with an under grip**

The next diagram shows in which direction the player plays the puck on – forwards and rearwards

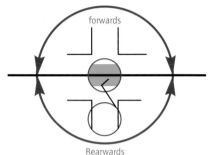

forwards

Rearwards

**Diagram 117**

### Face-off forwards – the correct technique

The face-off forwards is the simplest technical variation and the one that is used the most in the younger age groups. In practice, it is well known that the 8-11 year olds, when doing the face-off, only strike the puck and then in the easiest direction – forwards. In proper games with older players, and where the puck is deliberately played on in a particular direction, this version is seldom used. The use of this technique depends, of course, on the place for the drop-in, on the positions of the opponents, on the phase of play and on the number of players on the ice.

The individual techniques are similar to those listed for the principle way of doing the face-off. Unless otherwise indicated, the descriptions of the techniques are for players using the method of holding the stick in the left hand (for the left-handed). Reference is always made to the player in the diagrams with Number 7 on his shirt (the one with black socks).

## 9.3   Face-off Forwards – Straight Shot

This technique is very simple and is done either on the forehand or the backhand.

### Forehand shot directly from a face-off

From a basic position, the player turns himself partially forwards facing the goal (left-handed players with their right leg to the rear). The center of weight of the body is placed slightly over the right (left) leg and forwards. The stick is held in the under grip and the blade is placed as far to the left as possible in the white zone of the face-off spot.

The player is standing just as he would, just having received a pass. His concentration is on the puck and the target (the goal). The player tries to shoot the puck at goal without a pull back of the stick and immediately as it touches the ice (the player on the right in Diagram 118).

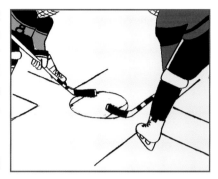

**Diagram 118**

Because of the low effectiveness of this technique it is only used in certain situations (end of a period or of the game, when there is little time left, when trying to create surprise or when an opponent is in a wrong position). Use of the technique in the attacking zone is possible, but it is limited by the way of holding the stick – the left-hander from the left side and the right-hander from the right side.

### Forehand shot after blocking the opponent's stick

The basic position is like the previous technique other than the position of the blade of the stick, which is now held as far to the right side of the white zone of the face-off spot as possible. It is important to concentrate on the movements of the opponent's stick.

When the opponent tries to play the puck, the player blocks it (only the tip of the blade or the whole blade) so that he can shoot the loose puck directly at goal. In Diagram 119, only the tip of the blade is blocked. In Diagram 120, the whole blade is blocked by the player on the left.

**Diagrams 119 & 120**

This technique is not so effective. Nevertheless, by comparison to the previous technique, the opponent's stick is not in the way of the puck. However, the technique is perfectly playable for a left-handed player against a left-handed player and equally so for right-handed against right-handed players. The reason for this is because the left-handed player can hardly direct the puck towards goal in the left of the attacking zone.

### Forehand shot after an individual action forwards

As already mentioned, techniques for the forward movements use the under grip. The player is coming from the left out of a normal position, as he would for a direct shot, and reacts to the puck in the referee's hand. When the puck drops out of his hand, the player tries to get behind the opponent onto the goal side and shoot the puck quickly

from behind him. The puck may not be played when it is still in the air and has not yet made contact with the ice – care must be taken to observe this rule. The direction of moving the puck on (either between the opponent's legs or in the direction that the player is moving himself) is up to the player to decide (see Diagram 121 – the player on the left).

**Diagram 121**

Coming in from the right, the technique is very similar. The left-hander comes in from a normal position and places the weight of his body forwards over his left leg (see Diagram 122 – the player on the left). It is possible to do the shot on the forehand as well as on the backhand.

**Diagram 122**

At the beginning, the player turns his blade upright so that he can strike the puck better (see Diagram 123 – the player on the left).

**Diagram 123**

The technique described places great demands on agility and speed of reaction. It can be used on both sides – from the left and from the right. For the left-hander, it is quicker when he comes from the left side, as he will be able to execute a shot immediately on the forehand side.

Nevertheless, the technique can be used from the right side in a manner that he can do a backhand shot or a quick changeover of the puck onto the forehand and then shoot. The players often play the puck out of the air, which is, however, not allowed in the rules. This technique can be used in situations when a defender, in his own defending zone, gets it onto the boards (see Diagram 124).

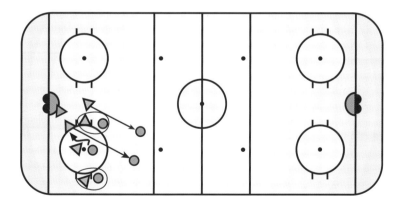

**Diagram 124**

### Backhand shot after an individual action

The face-off technique with a backhanded shot is not very accurate and therefore not used much. It can only be used in the attacking zone by right-handers coming in from the left and by left-handers coming in from the right.

The blade of the stick is placed as far as possible to the right (left) of the white zone of the face-off spot (in the next diagram – the player on the left). The player reacts to the puck and tries to strike it in the direction of goal.

**Diagram 125**

## 9.4   Face-off Forwards – Passing the Puck

The technique of playing the puck forwards with a pass is similar to the previous technique of facing off forwards with a shot afterwards. However, this method is not so critical regarding its accuracy and can be used in all the playing zones. Regarding the players' position when they face-off, it is better to play the puck to the rear to a teammate. Therefore, about 10% of all face-offs are played forwards. The choice and use of the technique is, once again, dependent on the tactics.

### Playing the puck forwards directly on the forehand

The technique is very similar to shooting directly after the face-off, but in this case it doesn't have to be so accurate.

In the basic position, the blade of the stick is placed to the left in the white zone of the face-off spot (for left-handers). Care must be take that the whole of the blade is on the ice when playing the puck.

This makes it possible to hit the puck easier. The player reacts to the movement of the puck as it leaves the referee's hand and tries to strike it forwards as soon as it touches the ice without pulling back the stick. Providing the player uses sufficient force, the opponent's stick will not prevent him hitting the puck (see Diagram 126 – the player on the right).

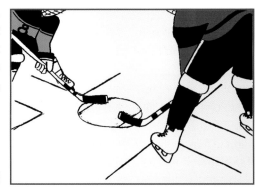

**Diagram 126**

**Playing the puck forwards on the forehand after blocking the opponent's stick**

Being able to play the puck forwards on the forehand after blocking the opponent's stick is also limited by the way the opponent holds his stick. This technique can only be used by left-handers against left-handers and right-handers against right-handers. A prerequisite for this is a quick reaction against the opponent's stick and sufficient strength in the arms to push his blade away.

The player starts in the basic position (with his skates also in the correct stance). The stick, held in the under grip, is placed in the right side of the white zone of the face-off spot. The player reacts, above all, to the movement of the opponent's stick and tries to prevent him striking it by making a quick forwards movement to the left. In this way the opponent's stick should be pushed away to the side followed by a quick movement of the stick to pass the puck forwards (see Diagram 127 – the player on the left).

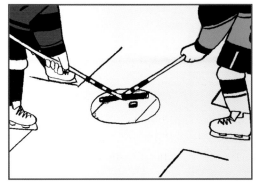

**Diagram 127**

### Individual action forwards on the forehand

The actions necessary for this technique have already been described in the method for a forehand shot after an individual action forwards. This technique can be used practically anywhere on the ice. After penetrating into the opponent's defending zone, no shot is made, but rather further action takes place according to the game situation.

This technique is not particularly effective. If it fails then a rapid and dangerous counter action can be provoked. Therefore it doesn't make sense to use this action in one's own defending zone. It is also important that the player taking the face-off tells his teammates what he is doing. In this way, they can possibly save the situation if something goes wrong (see Diagram 128 – the player on the left).

**Diagram 128**

### Playing the puck forward on the backhand

This technique is practically rarely used. More often, the technique of playing the puck on the backhand sends the puck rearwards. Nevertheless, playing the puck forward is also possible. The next diagram shows the possible angles that the puck can be played in for a left-hander.

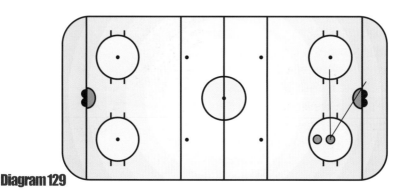

**Diagram 129**

### Playing the puck directly forwards on the backhand

This technique can be carried out using both the under and the over grip. It places a great deal of demand on the player's strength and the player must have a good feeling for playing the puck forwards or to the side on the backhand. The blade of the stick, therefore, has to be angled in the direction required.

The player is in the basic position with his right leg set out back a little and with the weight of his body centered over the left leg (for left-handers). The blade of the stick is placed as far as possible to the right in the white zone of the face-off spot. The player reacts to the puck and tries to strike it with a simple shot. At the same time he moves the weight of his body in the direction where he has played the puck, speeding up the action as he does it. It is essential to coordinate the movement of the body and the stick together. Playing the puck on remains the main aim (see Diagram 130 – the player on the left).

Because this technique is used when the puck does not necessarily have to be played accurately in a particular area, the player can force the opponent's stick to strike the puck.

### Playing the puck forwards on the backhand after blocking the opponent's stick

The basic position is the same as the previous technique. The blade of the stick is placed in the center of the white zone of the face-off spot. The player reacts to the puck and the opponent's stick movement. If the puck is still in the air, the player tries, by making a forward movement of his stick, to push the opponent's stick away from the spot where it is anticipated that the puck will land. He then plays the puck on into a particular area with a pass (see Diagram 130 – the player on the left). This technique requires a lot of strength.

### Individual action forwards on the backhand

In principle, this technique is the same as in the two previous ones. After playing the puck the player must not let himself be blocked by the opponent. He then moves off further in the direction that he has played the puck in (see Diagram 130 – the player on the left).

**Diagram 130**

## 9.5 Passing Back from the Face-off

These techniques are often used as, following success, the team is in possession of the puck already. They can be used in all the playing zones and areas on the ice. When using them, no shot at goal can be made. The puck can only be played rearwards. Theoretically, individual rearwards actions can be undertaken, however, they never really come about. In a game, the players practically never break away free rearwards. Nevertheless, situations can occur when a player, following a face-off, takes the puck to the rear and carries out an action further in that area.

Playing the puck back from the face-off on the forehand demands clever techniques and lightening execution. Forehand techniques can be used in practically all the playing zones with the exception of the own defending zone where the puck would be moving in the direction of the home goal.

**Playing the puck on directly rearwards on the forehand**

From the basic position, the blade of the stick is in the center of the white zone of the face-off spot. The player reacts to the puck and when it makes contact with the ice, he tries to strike as quickly as possible on the forehand. In order to pass the puck rearwards accurately, the player turns the tip of the blade into the forehand direction (for a left-hander to the right, for a right-hander to the left). He also makes a slight movement of his body at the same time in the opposite direction following the puck (see Diagram 131 – the player on the right).

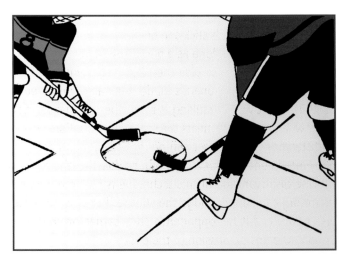

**Diagram 131**

**Playing the puck on rearwards on the forehand after blocking the opponent's stick**

This technique is very similar to the previous technique, but now played with a requirement for greater technical and individual tactical skill. It is used, above all, in situations when winning the puck is a certainty and when the opponent must not be able to get hold of the puck.

The player reacts to the puck as well as the opponent. When the puck is still in the air, the player tries to prevent the opponent getting into a better position with his stick for the face-off (see Diagram 132).

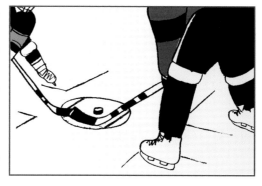

**Diagram 132**

Knowing the opponent's strong points leads to the choice of technique to be used. The player has to get to know when the opponent, using any particular technique to play the puck rearwards, doesn't exert so much strength, but concentrates more on the technique itself and speed. The stick movements are more complicated and take longer than a simple strike against the opponent's stick. The opponent cannot play the puck and so he is only able to pass it backwards.

Striking the opponent's stick can be done at any particular point along its length and at any time. This can be done as a quick strike against the tip of the blade (this is sufficient to get enough space to play the puck – see Diagram 119) or as a clash of the whole blade against the opponent's blade (this takes longer but is more sure – see Diagram 120). The best way of striking is to hit the opponent's stick about 5-10 cms above the point where the blade meets the shaft. This variation, however, requires greater strength and steadiness. The effect can be increased, then again, by turning the blade and the body movement inwards away from the direction the puck has been hit in.

One disadvantage of this technique is that the opponent (if he has registered the intention) can simply dodge the stick (either upwards or downwards). The player who was trying to hit his opponent's stick carries on in the backhand direction and the opponent gains possession of the puck.

### Individual action rearwards on the forehand

This variation is practically never seen in competitive games. Theoretically, it can be done, and therefore, it is covered here.

In practice, the technique begins mainly by the player turning in and blocking the opponent. A more rapid, but more strenuous way, in terms of the reaction and feeling required for the puck, is exactly like the technique of playing the puck directly on the forehand rearwards. The puck is then not played so hard and is only pushed backwards on the forehand side. The player must also not allow himself to be blocked by the opponent. He follows the puck and continues with the individual action. Usually, the face-off ends with the puck bouncing off in this direction. It depends on the player whether he prefers this technique or whether he prefers to block the opponent and leave the puck to a teammate (see Diagram 133).

**Diagram 133**

### Playing the puck directly rearwards on the backhand

All the rearward techniques in the face-off belong to the most popular preferred ones. They demand a lot more strength. They are quick and allow the puck to be brought under control.

The technique of playing the puck directly rearwards on the backhand can be done with the over as well as the under grip. The over grip is slower but stronger. For left-handers, the blade of the stick is as far as possible to the right of the face-off spot – for right-handers, the other way round. At the moment the puck hits the ice, the player tries to play the puck rearwards. In this case, it is more effective to use the so-called quick grip (see Methods). The player concentrates only on the puck, which he has to hit as it drops onto the ice. If the strike is made with enough force, the opponent's stick will not be able to stop it (see Diagram 134 – here the player is using the over grip; in Diagram 135 he is using the under grip).

**Diagram 134**

**Diagram 135**

## Playing the puck rearwards on the backhand after blocking the opponent's stick

This technique is slower, but surer. It demands a lot of strength and a quicker reaction to the puck and the opponent.

In the basic position, the blade of the stick is about in the center. Well before the puck contacts the ice, the stick is moved forwards towards the opponent's stick. The player tries to push the opponent's stick away from the face-off spot. As the puck hits the ice, the player pulls the stick closer and plays the puck rearwards (see Diagram 136).

**Diagram 136**

## Individual action rearwards on the backhand

The method for this technique is the same as was described for the individual action rearwards on the forehand. Important is a good feeling for playing the puck. When the player continues with the action on his own, he should not lay it too far forward. It is also important to know that when a right-hander blocks a left-hander (and vice versa); this is much more difficult and therefore, in practice, is not used.

161

### Methodical tips

- As already mentioned, the face-off is a very specific action, which is only carried out by the best players in the older age and top player groups. If one is aiming towards a championship, then a suitable method must be chosen for this age group, according to the skills already learned.

- From the very beginning of training, when everyone can already play, all the players try to have a go at the face-off. While they know of its existence, they don't have any knowledge of the rules, about taking up the basic position and how to hold the stick, and what positions the other players should be in etc.

- Sufficient attention must be devoted to practicing and perfecting the face-off in the weekly micro-cycles (periods of between 2-10 days – see "Hockey – Training for Kids"). This is valid for all age groups. Every member of the team should take part in the face-off, irrespective of playing position. It is only in older age groups that a specialization takes place.

- In the group of 6-8-year olds, the children should be advised that when there is a face-off, they should stay in their own half, because play will only be in individual playing zones. Practicing the technique and tactics of the face-off is for this age group still superfluous. It is sufficient, at this stage to give an explanation and a practical demonstration of the action. In the course of the game, all the players can have a go at the face-off.

- In the group of 9-10-year olds, play now takes place on the whole of the ice. In view of the fact that the face-off can take place in different playing zones and areas, the players must learn about the different positions that they have to take up in the defending and attacking zones. To start with, an explanation and a practical demonstration will suffice. The information should be given to all the players, irrespective of their playing position. For this age group, the face-off must not be seen as a fighting action. This is something the 11, 12, and 13 year olds start to learn about. Having learned the skills and as a supplementary to the training session, face-off training can be done for the 10 year olds at the end of the game play period.

- Because most of the players in this age group only strike out simply at the puck or the opponent's stick, they have to be taught that playing the puck is more important. It has to be repeated here that all the players have to practice the face-off.

## The correct technique

- First of all, here is a description of the basic position.
  The player is standing with feet wide apart and with his knees bent. The weight of the body is centered slightly over the tips of the skates. The player does not support himself by leaning on his stick on the ice (it is not a prop!). The stick is held by the upper hand at the pommel end and the lower hand holds it as one would when playing (with the under grip). The head is lifted up (it may not sink below the level of the referee's hand holding the puck) and the player is watching the puck in the referee's hand. The blade of the stick is placed in the white zone of the face-off spot (see Diagram 137).

The basic position is important for the player's stability and steadiness. For practicing this, the following is recommended:

The player stands at the face-off circle (first of all holding a stick, later without one) and a second player tries to push him away from this position. For older age groups, this exercise can be used in fitness and strength training for stability in tackling actions.

**Diagram 137**

- The player's reaction to the puck in the referee's hand is important. The player must concentrate on the puck and later also on the opponent's stick. The young players have to learn the skill of striking the puck at the first moment it makes contact with the ice. Later on, they must learn the correct position of the stick's blade and how their position and stance influence the direction of the puck when it is played on.

- The basic position is now put into practice, first of all combined with the simplest and most often used method – rearwards on the backhand – the so-called "quick grip". The player is standing with his legs slightly apart, legs bent at the knees, head lifted up and he is watching the puck in the referee's hand. He is holding the stick in the over grip in such a way that the upper hand is about 30 cms lower down and the lower hand, also gripping over the shaft, is about 20cms lower than the normal play mode. The player is not leaning with his stick on the ice. He simply holds it down in the white zone of the face-off spot (see Diagram 138).

**Diagram 138**

■ At this juncture, mention must be made of the defense technique that prevents the opponent playing the puck. This is a spoiling technique, which is used particularly before the blue line is reached and in the flanking areas of the defending and attacking zones.

The player adopts a position where the skates and the blade of the stick cover the widest area possible. The tips of the skates are pointing outwards. The stick is being held in an under grip position and the face of the blade is turned towards the opponent (see Diagram 139). The player does not have a very stable position in this stance and the effectiveness of the action is dependent on speed of moving the blade of the stick forwards.

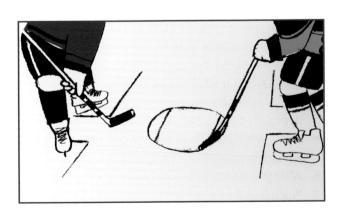

**Diagram 139**

## Tactical tips for face-off training

- The player should try to get well forward, because other players are not able to react quickly enough to the situation.
- If the face-off is lost, the opponent must not be allowed to push through forwards.
- In the defending zone, the puck must not be played in front of the home goal.
- Later on (possibly for players 12 years old) each player must get to learn how to play the puck in face-offs in all the various playing zones. Practice is done, firstly without an opponent and in various different directions.
- Training is done without an opponent.
- Training is done with a passive opponent (using both the under and over grips, forehand and backhand).
- Training with an opponent, games for three people – the players change round positions often.
- Training is incorporated into a game and the players then put what they have learned into practice.
- Later on, the trainer gives tactical tips for all the five players and for all playing positions in the individual playing zones. The simplest exercise is practiced by the group of five – the face-off using a technique playing rearwards that has already been learned. This is followed up by a shot in the attacking zone or with a pass to start an attack from the defending zone.

## Main mistakes

- While in the basic position, the player props himself up leaning on his stick.
- Wrong position of the legs and the stick.
- The legs are not bent at the knees and the legs are too close together.
- The player is bent forward too far and his head is below the level of the puck in the referee's hand.
- The player is not concentrating.
- The player adopts a basic position without checking the positioning of the opponent and his own teammates.
- The player doesn't watch the puck in the referee's hand.
- After the puck has been played, he remains passive.
- After the face-off, the player doesn't change back from the over grip.
- Practicing the face-off only with the center forwards and not all the other players.

## Exercise examples for face-off training

**1)** The trainer lays down the direction (target) that the puck is to be played in and a couple of players take up the best positions possible in order to do a face-off. One of the players tries to make the other lose his balance and steadiness. First of all, this is practiced without a stick and then later, with one.

**2)** The players stand in pairs opposite each other with the whole of the respective blades of their sticks touching each other. At a signal they try to knock each other off-balance only using the blades.

**3)** The players stand opposite each other in the face-off position. The puck is between the sticks. A third player stands where the puck should be played. At a command the face-off is played with a pre-determined winner. The other player only holds his stick passively on the ice during the play without countering.

**4)** One player stands at the face-off spot and the other tells him where he is to pass the puck. As required the player changes his position and the way he holds his stick. This way, the player learns to adjust himself to new situations.

**5)** The player is standing in the basic position just in front of the boards. On a signal he takes a lunging step forward and tries to "push the boards away".

**6)** There are three players – one player tries to win the face-off against the opponent, who is using various methods of holding the stick in different positions. Doing this he doesn't play the puck. The third player drops the puck in (changeover of players).

**7)** The players stand opposite each other with the puck on the ice between the sticks. On a signal they carry out a face-off tussle.

**8)** The players stand opposite each together with the puck on the ice between the sticks. On a signal, the players may only use their skates to play the puck. They can only use their stick to block the opponent.

**9)** One player tries to pass the puck with his stick and the other using only his legs (change of roles).

**10)** Once monthly, the players take part in a face-off competition.

# Game Combinations

P laying hockey demands that the players are always cooperating together, both in the attack as well as in the defense. Defending and attacking situations are mainly resolved by using game combinations.

A game combination is characterized by the close cooperation in a playing situation of two or more players taking part. Just as described in the individual playing actions, a distinction is made between attack combinations and defense combinations. Some of them can be used in all the playing zones, while others are used specifically in particular areas on the ice. Put in other words, it is very necessary that players cooperate together in order to place the opponent under pressure.

However, training for cooperation in game combinations should only be begun once the players can skate proficiently and they have learned the more important, individual playing actions for the defense and the attack. Unfortunately, it often happens that young players have to practice various complicated game combinations and patterns, and at the same time keep strictly to tactical maneuvers without having mastered good ice-skating techniques and the individual game techniques (with and without the puck) that go together with them.

This type of training brings a stagnation of the individual performance and at the same time suppresses the player's creativity, which, in any case, has negative results for the older age groups.

The type of skating exercises that teach the player how he should act relative to his own actions, what to do with the puck, and how to confront the opponent provide us with one of the basis for cooperation by the players in defense and in the attack.

However, this requires the participants to execute certain individual actions when on the attack and in defense. The players must be able to "read" the game.

In the hockey system, a difference is made between combinations done on the attack and those done in defense. For the 9-10 year olds, the children are only introduced to a few basic combinations and then exclusively to the simplest of them. The main emphasis must remain on the exercises mentioned already and on the individual skills and teamwork in defense and on the attack in 2:0, 3:0, 2:1, 3:1, and 2:2 (3:3) situations.

Practice has shown that solutions for game situations where several players are required to cooperate together in the attack as well as in defense, are too complicated for this age group and are therefore not suitable. Not all the players take part in the exercises, and on the other hand the coordination is only as good as their own personal skills.

At this age, the players learn to use the whole of the ice, how to maintain their own positions and then, first of all, later how they stand in for other teammates and back them up. One recommendable precursor for backing up actions like this is to use those exercises for movement without the puck when supporting the player with the puck.

It is mainly in 2:0, 3:0 and 3:1 (the attack triangle) situations that the players learn to use the whole width and length of the ice in a natural manner. The young players first receive basic instructions in training, for which the tactics involved are then converted into practical game situations. This way the players gain the necessary experience.

**Tips for training game combinations**

- When training for the game combinations, the preparatory part of the training session should include individual play actions that are important for the particular combination.
- The players should learn those basic principles for the combination by using simple exercises.
- Training begins, first of all, without an opponent (no resistance) and later with passive resistance.
- Later on, the exercises are practiced with an opponent, but always in such a manner so that the players can actually manage the combination without a problem (they should always have a certain advantage).
- After the basic principles have been mastered, the variations for the combination should be practiced so that the players get to learn what choices they have (tactics).
- The exercises should take place on the ice where they would normally occur in a game.
- After practicing a combination, a game concentrating on using this combination should be played.
- As already mentioned in this book, it is recommended that progressive training of the simpler combinations should also take place off the ice.

# 10.1 Attack Combinations

Some of the main elements for teamwork by the players in the attack are passing, receiving a pass and the ability to be able to breakaway free with the puck or without it. Of particular mention is the flat pass using the wrist shot on the move and high passes. The player holds his stick always in both hands on the ice. Also the players without the puck must always be on the move.

Practical experience shows that in the attacking actions one often uses game combinations that are based on certain basic principles.

### Principle – The passing and skating ("Give and Go") combination

This a basic combination for the attack, in which the player making the pass skates into a free area, where he will receive the puck passed back to him again. This combination can be used in all the playing zones (see Diagram 140).

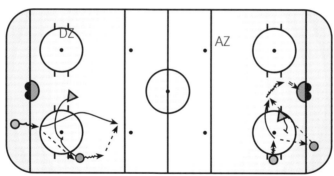

AZ = Attacking Zone / DZ = Defending Zone

**Diagram 140**

Another variation of this combination is based on the principle of passing and skating (see Diagram 141). The player doing the passing skates towards a teammate and passes the puck to him instead of trying to do a breakaway into a clear area. This variation demands good tactics. It is used where there is little room to move and is usually followed up by doing another combination (return passes, doing a drop pass and screening). It is recommended that this variation is done after the previous one has been learned.

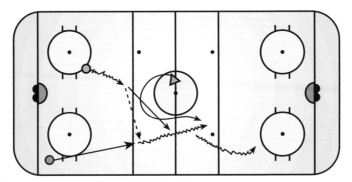

**Diagram 141**

## Methods

- The youngest players can use this combination in basic 3:0, 2:1 and 3:1 game situations.
- As described already, this combination requires a certain degree of technical know-how, particularly being able to pass and receive a pass on the move.
- The players practice doing passes standing still and moving along slowly.
- Then, 2:0 situations are practiced without any opposition. Suitable exercises for this can be seen in the next diagram.

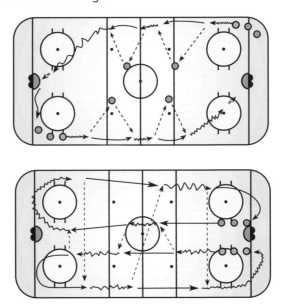

**Diagram 142**

- Exercises on the move (see Diagram 143) doing a pass between each pair of cones.

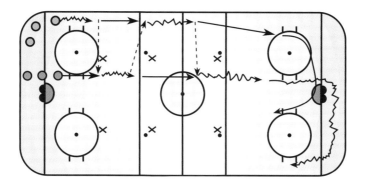

**Diagram 143**

- Combination (passive, active) with opponents in all the playing zones (see Diagram 144).

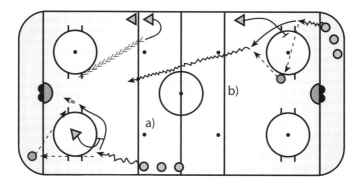

**Diagram 144**

### Main mistakes

- After doing the pass the player stands still.
- The player approaches his teammate blind (without being able to see him).
- Passes are not accurate.

### Principle – combinations using the 'crossing' method

This variation is based on players crossing over as they change position. It is used in 2:1, 3:2, 2:2 and 3:3 situations. The main role is played by the player without the puck skating on to the puck. It is used in all phases of the attack and when pressing forwards in the attacking zone. It is often combined with other combinations such as the return pass, doing a drop pass and screening. If the forwards are being closely marked, for example in the defending zone by the blue line, they can breakaway from the opponent by doing a crossing maneuver and then take on a pass. The combination is very successful against good position defense by the opponents in the area between the blue line and the neutral line in the attacking zone. The next diagram shows how practical its use is in a game.

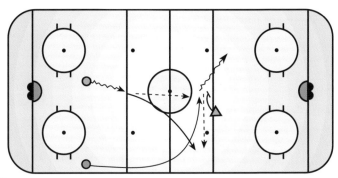

**Diagram 145**

## Methods

■ Theoretical explanation combined with a practical demonstration (by another player or using a video).
■ Preparatory exercises for the combination – it is recommended that the exercises for receiving the puck and passing are done alternately on the forehand and the backhand with a change of position (eventually also with a drop pass) (see Diagram 146).

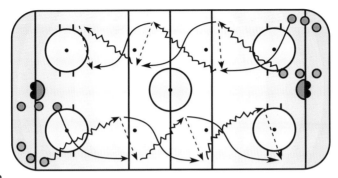

**Diagram 146**

- Training of the crossing maneuver without any resistance by the opposition and finishing off with a drop pass (see Diagram 147).

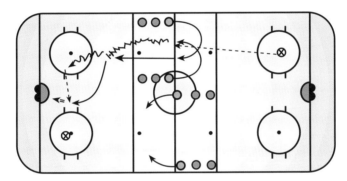

**Diagram 147**

- Practice with passive and active resistance (see Diagram 148).

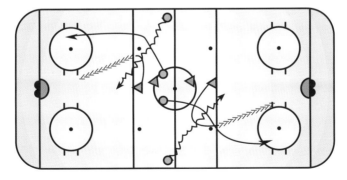

**Diagram 148**

### Main mistakes

- The players have no visual contact with each other.
- When crossing they stop skating.
- The player without the puck crosses over in front of the player with the puck.

### Principle – combinations using the 'drop pass' and return pass methods

The players have to learn the difference between a drop pass and a return pass.

The drop pass (where the player leaves the puck behind for the teammate to play on) is a combination based on players changing places. A major role is played by the player with the puck and the player without the puck reacts to the former's moves. The combination requires to be done accurately and with optimum timing. The player must never drop pass to a teammate who is "blinded" from the maneuvers. The follow-on movements of the player who does the drop pass are also important (screening, breaking away into a clear area etc.). A typical example in a 2:1 situation is where the player with the puck is moving forward against an opposing defender. Shortly before he reaches the opponent, he does the drop pass and screens the defender's field of view or continues the movement with a change of position. Most important of all is the requirement for the player without the puck to move forward to gather the puck at the correct moment (see Diagram 149).

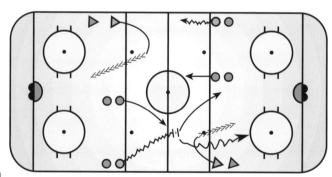

**Diagram 149**

The drop pass is often used when building up the attack. This is in cases where the puck is behind the goal and the defender is in front of his goal. In addition to using the drop pass behind the goal, and according to the game situation, the use of the return pass can also be used in combination with it (see Diagram 150).

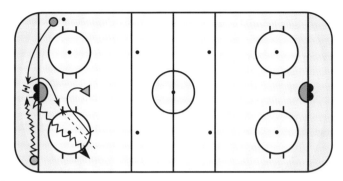

**Diagram 150**

The return pass is very important for one's own play. It can play a role in building up or developing the attack, when reorganizing it or concluding the attack. From a technical point of view, the return pass must come as a surprise, be accurate and above all occur at the last second. It is also important that the passer must get involved in play straight away after passing. These build-up combinations using the return pass are often combined with other attack combinations, particularly the crossing maneuver and screening (see Diagram 151).

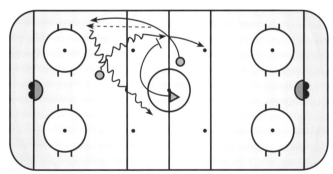

**Diagram 151**

## Methods

- One prerequisite for learning these combinations is the mastering of the pass on the forehand and the backhand and receiving a pass.
- The player should only use the return pass when he is sure his teammate is ready (never pass 'blind').
- Training is started by using simple preparatory exercises (drop pass) (see Diagram 152).

175

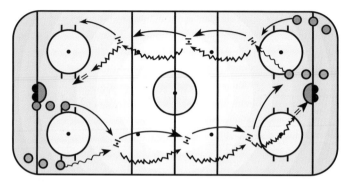

**Diagram 152**

- First of all, training is done at slow speed and without any opposition.
- Later on, the exercises are speeded up and the opponent defends passively.
- Lastly, the exercise is perfected and play situations in a game are included.

### Main mistakes

- The players are not in eye contact with each other.
- The player passes 'blindly'.
- Inaccurate passes or drop pass (the player doesn't do a drop pass, but passes it in another direction).
- The player, who has done the passing, doesn't continue to actively partake in play.

### Principle – combination using the 'screening' method

This combination is really only suitable for older age groups, nevertheless, its use in play is often made in attack combinations, which have already been covered in this book. Therefore, at this point, this combination will be included here.

Screening is the cooperation of players where the player without the puck limits and hinders (within the rules) the play being done by the defender, thus allowing his teammate the opportunity of carrying out better control of the puck. Screening can be very successfully employed in 5:5 situations, with man advantage 5:4 and in a face-off in practically all areas and in any possible game situation with a different number of players. Combined with the drop pass, the return pass and the crossing maneuver, this combination provides a good variation to solve man advantage 2:1, 3:2 situations as well as in level situations 2:2 as 3:3.

Screening, which is often called blocking, is a tactical variation, which the player with the puck uses to secure room for his puck handling. This means that it is not a tackle, as it is often wrongly misrepresented. Nowadays, the technique used is laid down very strictly in the ice hockey rules.

For the player doing the screening, in relation to the opponent and his teammate with the puck, it is important that he keeps on the move and at the appropriate moment he makes a movement or changes his position so that he creates an obstacle for the opponent. The screening technique does not only concentrate on the opponent, but also on his stick, which in some situations is a simpler and more effective alternative. The screening player is ready, eventually to take on the pass (dependent on the reaction of the defending player) (see Diagram 153).

**Diagram 153**

**Methodical tips**

- Description of the action relative to the ice hockey rules.
- Practical demonstration on the ice (or video).
- Preparatory exercises using passive resistance by the opposition (see Diagram 154).

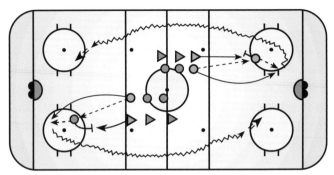

**Diagram 154**

- Practice with active opponent.
- Practice in the various playing zones and areas – attack build-up, development and conclusion – from left and right (see Diagram 155 – exercise for starting an attack using screening).

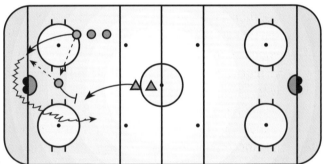

**Diagram 155**

- Practicing various play variations.

### Main mistakes

- The player has no visual contact with the opponent or his own players.
- The player screens too early – this is equivalent to illegal interference.
- The player screens too late thus permitting the opponent to defend effectively.
- The player loses contact with the opponent too early and thus permits him to check the player with the puck again.
- The player concentrates only on the opponent and fails to screen his stick.

## 10.2 Defense Combinations

It can also be said that it is important that, for successful training in defense combinations, individual defensive actions and ice-skating techniques must have been mastered. The tips for training game combinations, which are listed at the beginning of this chapter about game combinations, are also valid here.

For the defense, the system of ice hockey makes a distinction between five basic combinations. In the 9-10 year old age group, only a few of these are practiced and then only the basic ones. Experience shows that the complicated cooperation required by players in defense is not yet suitable for this age group. On the other hand, where combinations are preferred, such as those that have a direct connection to individual actions in a situation, and there is a basic attack combination variation suitable, they can be used as imagined by this age group.

**Taking on the opponent**

This is about the cooperation between players where the defenders take on the opponents in marking the free areas as well as doing man marking. This combination demands a lot of communication between the defenders and quite a few tactical skills. This is why the youngest players are only taught the basic principles of such combinations to start with. From the defense point of view, these combinations can be used in 2:2, 3:3 and eventually 3:2 situations as well as in a game 5:5 situation.

Taking on the opponent is done for two main reasons. In both, intercommunication and anticipation of play amongst the players are absolutely essential. In the first instance, this is in situations where the defenders require to take on the attacking players in order to facilitate further defense tactics (2:2 situation – Situation in the neutral zone   see Diagram 156).

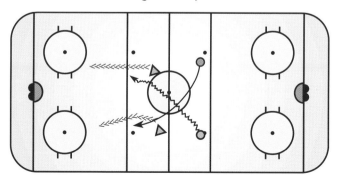

**Diagram 156**

179

In the second instance, this is in situations where the defender temporarily loses the tackle and his teammate takes on all marking work against the opponent (for example in the defending zone – lost tackle in the corner of the ice – see Diagram 157).

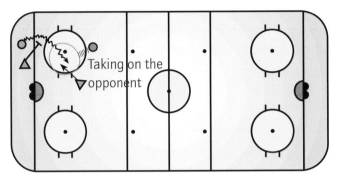

Taking on the opponent

**Diagram 157**

### Methodical tips

- Theoretical description of the action and a practical demonstration on the ice (or a video).
- Preparatory exercises for taking on by the player without the puck 2:2 and 3:3 (for example breaking away free 2:2, the defenders take on the opponent when given a command).
- Practicing slowly.
- Exercises for taking on the opponent – the defenders take on their opponents together (see Diagram 158).

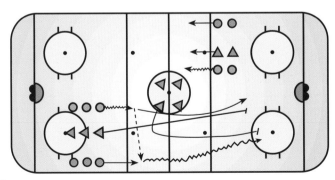

**Diagram 158**

- Training is done in a confined area or zone (in the neutral zone for example – see Diagram 159).

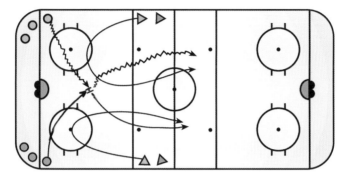

**Diagram 159**

**Main mistakes**

- Coordination of movements between the players is insufficient – both are marking the same opponent.
- Exchange of verbal communication between the players is missing.
- After taking on the opponent, he is not marked closely enough.
- After a lost tackle, the player doesn't immediately involve himself in active play.

**Man marking**

In this type of combination, the defenders mark the opponents very closely. Aim of this action is to limit the attacker's passes and to stop him being able to break out free into a clear area. Communication between the players is also important here. If the opponent with the puck is able to play round a defender, the next defender available must be in a position to take him on. A player, who loses his tackle, must begin to mark a free opponent as quickly as possible.

The combination is used particularly in a 2:2 and 3:3 situation. In a 5:5 situation it is used in specific phases of play (end of a period, after the face-off etc.). From a defense point of view, we are dealing here with very strenuous and aggressive playing variations. They call for quick starts from good and skilled skaters. They must be physically, strongly developed, be excellent at anticipation and very conscientious. Marking the opponent is done by using a perfected technique in tackling.

For the 9-10 year old age group, these types of combinations are only used to practice the improvement of the tackling technique in a 1:1 situation. Even then, they are used to practice the possibility of taking on the opponent from the defense point of view. In no way should this be confused with man marking, simply because of the combination.

### Methodical tips

- Explanations and a practical demonstration (best using video films).
- The preparatory exercises suitable for this are ice-skating exercises in pairs with and without the puck (copy cat exercises mimicking what the partner does etc.).
- Simple preparatory exercises with some limitations imposed on the center forwards (see Diagram 160 a, b).

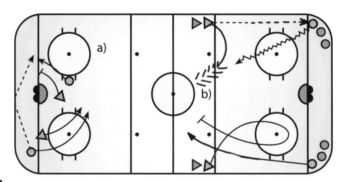

### Diagram 160

- Practicing 2:2 and 3:3 situations in a confined space.
- Playing 2:2 and 3:3 in a playing zone, but sideways with two goal mouths.

### Main mistakes

- The player has his back towards the puck and loses his overview of the play.
- Not enough effort put into the tackling action.
- The player is marking the opponent only with his stick.
- The player is marking only the opponent and not his stick as well.
- The player commits illegal actions (blocking, hooking, slashing with the stick etc.).

**Securing space**

This term means that the players cooperate together in defense and use their movements and positioning to secure an area and space to play in the zone so that a teammate can more easily check the opponent. This can be seen as providing support for the cooperative form of checking the puck handling opponent. The player, who is securing space for his teammate, must always be ready for further defensive actions or combinations. In cases where a tackle is made on an opponent dribbling the puck by a checking defender, then the player securing space must be able to react at the right moment and take the puck on. If the defender loses the tackle, then he also has to take on the opponent immediately himself. Combinations, which are based on securing space increase the pressure of time and space on the opponent dribbling the puck and at the same time provide an opportunity for doubling-up or taking on. It is important that the player undertaking the securing of space always has a good overview over the situation. He has to constantly watch what the opponents without the puck are doing, not let it get to a fight about the area being played in and be prepared to react to a pass. The player carrying out securing space must always be on the 'defensive side' i.e., between the puck and his own goal.

For this age group, the young players must definitely be taught this defensive combination – of course dependent on the skills they have managed to accomplish up until now.

This type of combination can be used in practically any of the playing zones. Diagram 161 illustrates the situation where the opponent with the puck is in the corner of the home defensive zone.

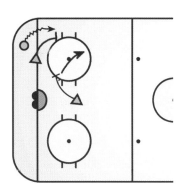

**Diagram 161**

**Methodical tips**

- Practical demonstrations with explanations of the theory.
- The player securing space must always be on the 'defensive side' (between the puck and his own goal).
- Simple exercises in a 1:2 situation, with the defender being screened, are shown in the next diagram.

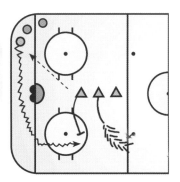

**Diagram 162**

- The defenders move in the direction of the puck.
- Practice of the players' movements, according to the opponent's position (the center forward without the puck and the puck handling player watch each other and chase in 1:2 and in 2:2 situations – see Diagram 163).

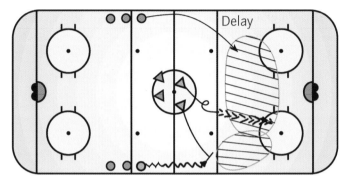

**Diagram 163**

- Game situations in individual playing zones.
- Using the combination in a game.

### Main mistakes

- The player securing space is too far away or too close to the checking teammate.
- The player has his back to the puck.
- The player is too wound up in the play and doesn't watch what is happening on the remainder of the ice (behind him).
- The player is not in a position between the puck and his own goal.
- The player is not prepared for further defensive actions (doubling-up, taking on, checking).

# Game Situations

T he basic variations of game situations for the age group of 9-10 year olds are contained in particularly the man advantage cases of 2:0, 3:0, 2:1, and 3:1 as well as the level situations 2:2 and 3:3. The level situations, first of all, improve the individual playing capability and are based on the technical solution found in a one-on-one situation in the attack and the defense. In no way should conscious practice of man marking be carried out, as this is very much connected with fitness training in older age groups.

The main principles of training and for the improvement of playing capability in the attack are:

■ The attack action is done at the fastest speed.

■ Every attack action is directed at the opponent's goal.

Much attention should be placed on cooperation in game situations of 2:0. Passes, receiving the puck, breaking out free with and without the puck, starting off in clear areas including shooting, combinations, "give and go", crossing, drop passes and return passes are all playing actions, which are contained in these situations and which have to be constantly improved.

The 2:0 situation should be practiced skating forwards and backwards as well as when skating cross-overs and changing direction. After mastering these, simple exercises with changes of playing positions (the player skates in the direction where he has passed) follow up, and, time and time again, the basic combination of "give and go" is practiced. These exercises without the presence of resistance (i.e., any opposition) get the young players into the habit of how they should perform correctly i.e., their own efforts, what to think about regarding the puck and the playing area – it's all about movement exercises.

The individual exercises, which depend on cooperation when passing, consist of several variations. The next diagram shows different variations of cooperation in a 2:0 situation.

- Passes and dribbling.

- Direct passes backwards and forwards without dribbling.

- Passes with a feinting movement or dodging maneuver.

- One player passes when skating backwards, the other when he is skating forwards.

- Passing when skating forwards and backwards, crossing at the same time.

- Crossing and doing a drop pass.

- Passing after carrying out a feinting movement in the opposite direction.

- A feinting movement in the opposite direction, crossing and then doing a drop pass.

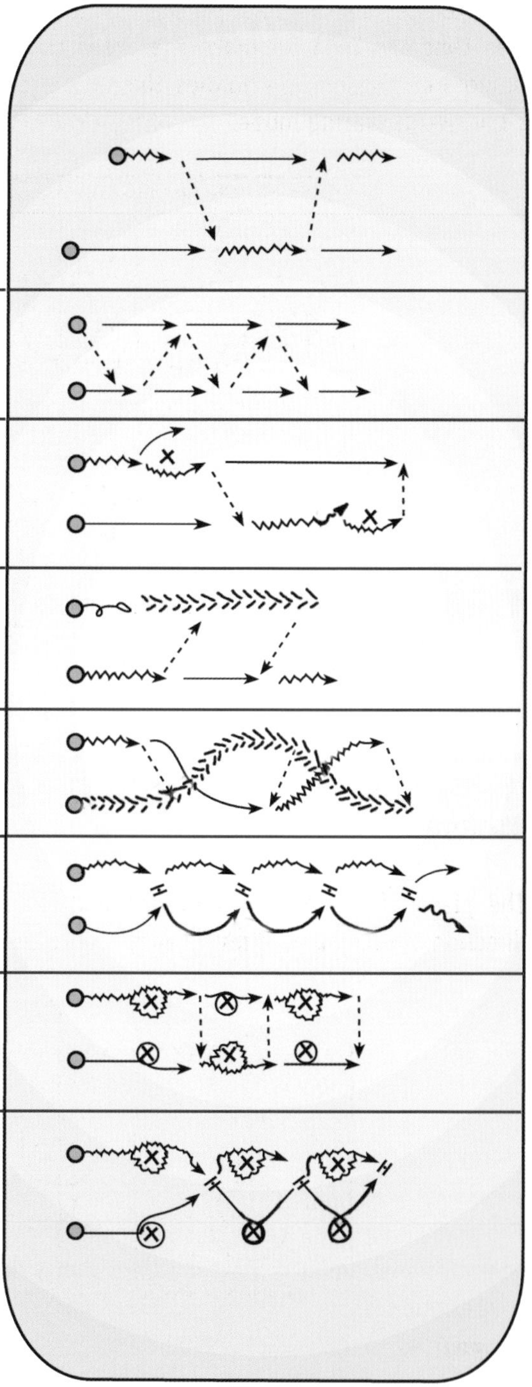

**Diagram 164**

The exercises can be done on the whole of the ice or only in certain playing zones (see Diagram 165). To make the exercises more difficult, agility elements can be brought in; passing over hurdles, the puck is received after a quick turn forwards from a backwards skating mode.

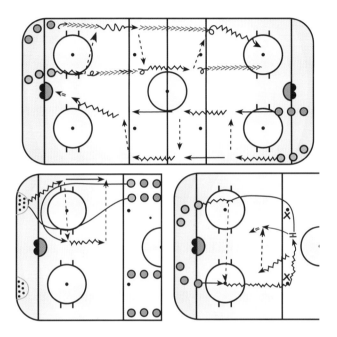

**Diagram 165**

The players learn how to move correctly in the attacking half of the ice (in the direction of the goal and not towards the corners) (see Diagram 166).

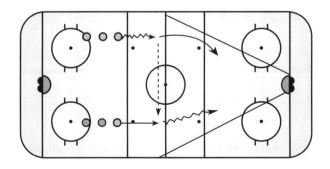

**Diagram 166**

To conclude an attack action in a 2:0 situation, the players learn two basic variations. The first is where both players are skating along level with each other and aiming towards goal. Each of them skates towards "his side" of the goal. Depending on the position of the goalie, the player with the puck aims at the unguarded corner or he passes the puck at the last moment to his teammate to shoot. Passing the puck at exactly the right moment is the secret of shooting successfully. Passing the puck too soon gives the goalie the advantage that he can change his position and react to the shot. On the other hand, a pass made too late doesn't give the receiver any opportunity to shoot properly and allows the goalie to stop the puck with a save. In order to be able to carry out a rebound shot (where given the chance) the players remain hovering in front of the goal (see Diagram 167).

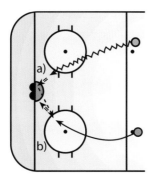 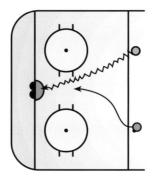

**Diagram 167**

In 2:1 situations, the opponent's resistance is got past by all the attacking players cooperating together. This type of situation (with the exception of man marking) arises in all phases of play and in all the playing areas. It is inseparable from playing in situations with man advantage.

An essential prerequisite for training in the attack phase is to have perfect cooperation in the 2:0 situation. Very often the solution concentrates only on the cooperation of the players and the possibility to get past the opponent alone is forgotten about. In practice, exercises are only done in the neutral and attacking zones and the game situation for the build-up to the attack is often neglected. Situations are mainly resolved by using various attack combinations (the most important of these are described further in the following sections). Individual exercises are carried out in confined areas as well as on the whole of the ice.

The players learn how to do the combination with the principle of the "give and go" action. It is important to remember to pass at the correct moment and then accelerate into a clear area for the return pass. As an example, the case of starting an attack from the defending zone can be quoted. First of all, the exercise is done with passive opposition (see Diagram 168).

A similar exercise can be done also in the attacking zone where play comes in from the corner (see Diagram 169). The main emphasis in this exercise is not only the way the passer accelerates but also on the movements done by the player receiving the pass. When the player moves correctly, he can disrupt the opponent's attack.

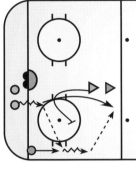

**Diagram 168**

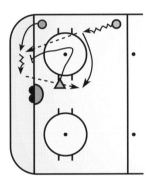

**Diagram 169**

In the combination of the "give and go", the player with the puck is attacked by the opponent and at the very moment when he is front of him, he passes the puck to his teammate (who should be level with him or not too far in front). The player making the pass moves off in the direction that the second player breaks away. At the moment, when the opponent attacks the player with the puck, the first player receives a return or a drop pass. For this, the acceleration of the first player is again important (see Diagram 170).

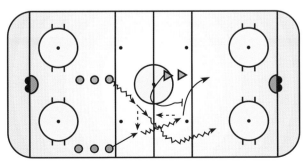

**Diagram 170**

In a clear area (for example crossing the blue line) the players learn to use the principle of "crossing and drop passing" (return passing) to beat the opponent. It is important to know which player moves first when crossing. If we are dealing with a drop or return pass, then the first to move is the player with the puck. He dribbles the puck in the direction of the goal and as he crosses the blue line, he changes the direction he is skating in. The player without the puck also indicates that he is skating further on making a breakaway towards the goal, but then changes direction so that he can gain time and space to receive a pass and increase speed. After doing a drop pass, the players speed up play and skate on towards the goal. An example of this is in Diagram 171. It is practiced from both the left and the right side as well as using puck handling down the axis of the ice and along the boards.

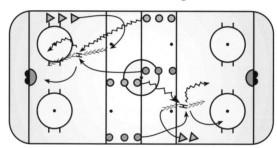

**Diagram 171**

When the first player doesn't have the puck in his possession, in older age groups, the principle of screening the opponent can be used. Very often, the crossing method is used just before or beyond the blue line (when penetrating into the attacking zone watch out for off-side). When using crossing or a drop pass, the situation can be resolved further by employing two variations. The player with the puck either carries on with the action or shortly after crossing he passes the puck to a second player once he has got past the defender. This variation is technically more difficult. In the case where the player with the puck is a left-hander and he is playing from the right-hand side in the direction of the axis of the ice, then he has to do this movement on the backhand (see Diagram 172).

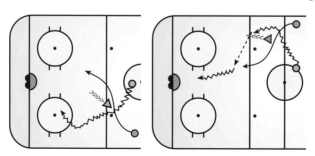

**Diagram 172**

When concluding a 2:1 situation, the same principles are used as when cooperating in a 2:0 situation. The player with the puck should aim for the side of the goal and the player without the puck reacts to the first player.

When the defender is skating slowly and maintains a position in front of the goal, the player increases his skating speed (again towards one side of the goal) in order to be able to receive a pass from his teammate. In the case that the pass comes in late he brakes short of the goal so that the player can still shoot in the puck (see Diagram 173).

When the defender is skating slowly and maintains a position in front of the goal, the player with the puck on the central axis can penetrate in behind the defender and finish off the action himself. In this case, the player without the puck changes his direction on the axis of the ice and brakes some way from the goal in order to receive any possible pass or to carry out a rebound shot (see Diagram 174).

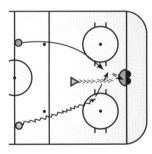
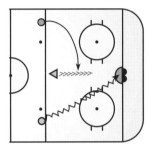

**Diagram 173**                                    **Diagram 174**

From a defense point of view, the resolution of a 2:1 situation must be explained and practiced. In practice, however, it often happens that the trainer concentrates only on the cooperation in the attack and neglects the defense.

In an attack action through the center of the ice (see Diagram 175) there are certain rules.

■ The defending player skates backwards down the central axis (imaginary lines to the goal net posts) and keeps his eye on the forward. So that he can maneuver better, he skates using a broad split-legged stance. He is holding the stick in one hand and tries to block any pass. Marking his man closely and using his stick he pushes the opponent into a less favorable position in the direction of the boards.

- The player keeps as close contact as possible with the opponent and tries to slow down the attack action.
- The defender skates at the same speed as the attacking forward.
- The player must not let the attacking player without the puck get behind him.

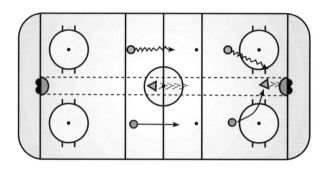

**Diagram 175**

In a situation when the opposition manages to get into the defending zone, the player maintains close contact with the attacking forwards and tries to push them away from the central axis. At the same time he skates at the same speed as them and tries to slow down the attacking movement so that his teammates can get back. He stays constantly prepared to block a pass and using stick movements, he puts the opponents under pressure. In the event that the player with the puck carries out a shot, he has to screen the player, who moves off towards the goal to carry out any possible rebound shot. This is usually the center forward without a puck.

The player continues to defend hard up to the last moment. In no way should he let himself be pushed back close to the goalie. Earlier training recommendations said that when in the immediate vicinity of the goal, the defender should screen the opponent without the puck, leaving the goalie to take care of the player with the puck. In modern ice hockey this has limited validity. This is proved in top game performances. Therefore, it is also not advisable to emphasize this game option.

Cooperation between the players in a 3:0 situation is first practiced after having mastered the 2:0 situation. Cooperation between three players is a little more complicated, above all when the action involves more than one defender. This situation demands good passing and receiving skills on the forehand and the backhand. For this age group, it is not a good thing in a 3:0 situation that the players change round during the action. The players have to be made familiar with their playing positions (in the breadth and depth). In the home half of the ice, the whole width of it should be used. Compared with this, in the attacking half of the ice, the actions should be always made in the direction of the goal (see Diagram 176).

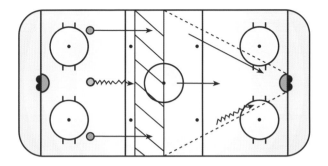

**Diagram 176**

At this point, the principles of forming an attack triangle are described, but not in a 3:0 situation, rather in a game situation 5:5. When concluding the action, it should be directed at goal, and where the situation permits, the players remain in the vicinity of the goal (in the same way as the principles in a 2:0 situation). The attack triangle demands being able to do follow-up shots at goal and the ability to get back quickly into a defensive position (see Diagram 177).

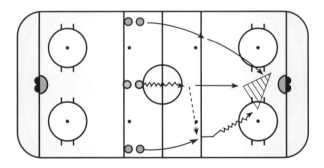

**Diagram 177**

Some 10-11 year olds are capable at the end of the competition period of changing round in the conclusion of a 3:0 action and play as they would in an older age group in a 3:2 (3:3) game situation. The player on the central axis in front of the blue line passes the puck out sideways to a teammate and then skates on down the center in the direction of the goal. The player with the puck moves with his eyes on the target and the player without the puck plays as the center forward (see Diagram 178). In this way, the triangular formation of the players and stopping in front of the opponent's goal are important factors. The players must be taught the importance and role of the player at the tip of the triangle (the shooter and the first defending forward).

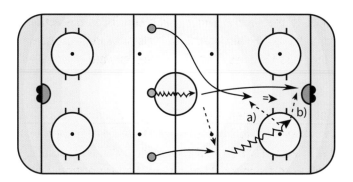

**Diagram 178**

For this age group, cooperating in a 3:1 situation represents, in a way, a summarization and a conclusion of the skills learned and mastered in the situations (2:0, 2:1 and 3:0) covered so far.

The basics and main principles are the same as in a 3:0 situation. It must always be remembered that, attack actions in the attacking half of the ice must always be in the direction of the goal. When developing the attack, having sufficient breadth of playing positions (attack triangle) is an important factor. It often happens that the players without the puck skate too far forward and stand, as a result, with their backs to the player with the puck. This will cause the cooperation to be somewhat limited. The player with the puck will then get into a classic 1:1 situation, which is not what is wanted in this case.

The conclusion of a 3:1 situation can be played as a simple, but nevertheless extremely effective, action just as it is in a competition game. At the end of these situations, in practice play, it is quite clear that the variations that leave out superfluous changing round of positions are the ones that are preferred. When training the conclusion of an attack, the player on the boards (winger or 'wingman') will receive the puck well before he reaches the blue line and then come in towards his goal post target in the attacking zone. The center forward skates to his position in order to be able to receive a return pass. The second winger with the puck skates as fast as possible towards the goal and thus an attack triangle is formed by these players.

For a successful conclusion of this action, the inclusion of the winger with the puck into play is a decisive movement. Dependent on the position of the defending player, he passes the puck to the second winger, who concludes the action. If he doesn't receive the puck, he has to remain at a certain distance from the goal, in order to be able to receive any possible pass from the center forward or score with a rebound shot.

The second variation after a penetration in the attacking zone consists of a quick pass back to the center forward (to the player at the tip of the attack triangle). This player concludes the action with a shot (when the defender is standing too close to his goal) or he passes to a winger standing in a better position. Quick anticipation of play by the center forward in this type of action is important. The decision he takes whether to shoot or pass (and to which player) is an important factor (see Diagram 179).

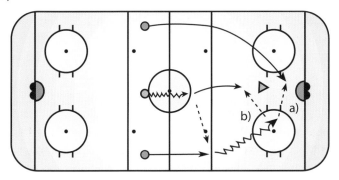

**Diagram 179**

Because of the cooperation required in level situations 2:2 and 3:3, the attacking and defending players should play only using the technique form of 1:1 tackling stressed so far. When the defending player loses the puck against an attacking forward, the other defending players have the possibility of taking on the opponents in such situations. The exercises for this are covered in the next chapter.

Training of individual game situations should not be at the expense of the individual creative skills by the players. The player must always be ready to conclude on his own any situation he encounters. This is mainly the case for times when the defending opponent makes a mistake.

# Team Play Organization on the Attack and in Defense

For this age group, the young players should only be kept informed about team play organization. It should not be seen as deliberate training for certain team play systems in the attack and in defense. The fundamentals consist of the individual skills already learned and the resolution of various game situations using simple combinations. All the preparatory exercises are done without an opponent present.

### Team play organization in defense

The attention here is on the basic formation of the players in the attack and defense, concentrating on a 2-1-2 layout. The players are responsible for a certain part of the ice, which is determined by their layout. The formation of an attack triangle is stressed, as this is also the basis for the defending triangle when the puck is lost.

In the attacking zone, checking the opponents is essentially carried out by two players. The player nearest to the puck checks the opponent dribbling the puck. The role of the defending forward in defending the center of the ice is undertaken by either the last player (this springs out of the layout of the attack triangle) or the center forward. Playing, by using a center forward, is simpler for this age group and more suitable with younger players.

In the defending zone, the responsibility for a particular area is described in a 2-1-2 layout (see Diagram 180). The layout of the defending players and the forwards is explained.

DZ = Defending Zone / AZ = Attack Zone

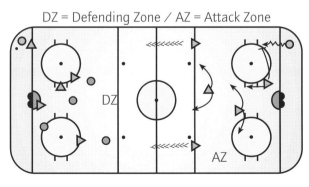

**Diagram 180**

### Team organization in the attack

Simple exercises for starting a progressive attack out of the defense form one of the main themes. These exercises, together with exercises in passing, breaking out free without the puck and exercises for resolving game situations with combinations (2:0, 3:0), form a single unit. The exercises develop the ability of the player to orient himself on the ice relative to the puck and his own teammates. Practice is done in correct (frontal), timely and exact starts to get the puck. Where the exercises for starting an attack by the players on the defensive positions are begun, it is advantageous that these players bring in other actions beforehand.

An example is the exercise where the defender shoots from the blue line, turns round to skate backwards and only then receives the puck, which he passes on to the attacking forward or to the second defender (see Diagram 181). When two players carry out the exercise, the second player should also practice this action.

Later, exercises involving all 5 players can be employed, but always without the presence of any opposition (see Diagram 182). In these exercises it is about learning and improving the skills and not about pressure play.

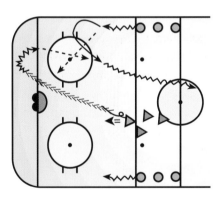

**Diagram 181**

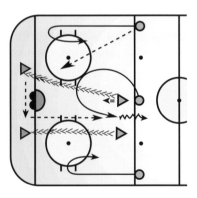

**Diagram 182**

Depending on the skills achieved by the 10-11 year old players, they can do exercises to practice the long pass. However, only the preparatory exercise forms are suitable (see Diagram 183).

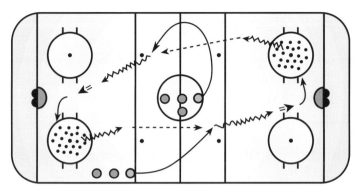

**Diagram 183**

### Play with man advantage

The players are taught the basic principles of this kind of defensive play. The team with man advantage (i.e., a team with at least one more player on the ice than the opposition) has better chances of scoring a goal. There are no exercises for starting an attack or concluding it where there is a man advantage. Any exercise consists of either an individual action or a pass (see playing 5:5). In the attacking zone, the same play as in a 5:5 situation with two players on the blue line is called for.

### Short-handed play

Learning to play short-handed (i.e., a team with less players on the ice than the opposition) requires a demonstration without any preparation of system or methods etc. Play in a short-handed situation doesn't necessarily mean the other team will have success in scoring a goal. The short-handed team has to be very much on guard and use all the skills they have learned to best effect (particularly blocking and stopping shots). The layout of a team in this situation is to have two players forward and two players in the rear in the defending zone.

# 13 Organizational Possibilities for Play

**P**laying is a very suitable medium, not only for improving movement skills, but also for the development of the ability to move (fitness) in older age groups. Play should be practical and varied, employing all possible forms and variations. Play is best done, similar to play for the 6-8 year olds, by using the ice crosswise in the playing zones and using lightweight pucks to improve puck handling. Playing at this age (9-10 years old) teaches the players the defensive actions as well as attacking actions. Emphasis is placed on employing close-quarter play, play in the different zones, along the boards, in the face-off circles, in the corners and on the lines etc., with different numbers of players (from 1:1 up to 5:5).

For the perfection of the skills learned; "playing is a better teacher than the trainer himself".

It is generally well known that those trainers, who work with children, use a large palette of little games in training. Despite this, in this chapter we summarize the possibilities of organizing play from the viewpoint of available space and the number of players and as generally, internationally accepted.

**Playing on the whole of the ice**

Play can be constructed so that it is either done as flowing play (the trainer doesn't intervene – he merely observes that the rules are maintained) or it is played as a controlled game (the trainer intervenes and gives corrections). In this age group, however, it is recommended that flowing play is interrupted as little as possible by the trainer. Changeovers of players can be done in at least two variations.

The players changeover after a break in play, similar to the way it is done in a competitive game. The second variation is to changeover on a signal from the trainer and where the next players come onto the ice during play (called a 'change on the fly'). In line with a prearranged rule, the players leave the puck alone or play it off in a particular direction (into a corner, at goal, into the center circle etc.,) when a signal is given. The time allowed for the changeover is between 30-45 seconds.

During the training session, the basics of cooperation (use of combinations) not only in the attack (starting an attack from the defending zone) as well as in defense (layout 2-1-2) are being worked on. Here it is recommended that play is directly taken on from the exercises to actually doing the moves in the form of play. For example, one moves from the action of starting and developing an attack 5:0 in the defending zone straight on with flowing play, 5:5 into the neutral zone. This doesn't mean of course, that in the training session any suitable preparatory or play exercises for learning cooperation are left out.

**Play in the individual game zones**

Play in the individual game zones should also be covered for this age group. As with the 6-8 year old players, mini-hockey can be played (4:4, 5:5) using the playing zones and play can be organized either 1) according to the number of players or 2) by using regular changeovers or 3) by playing longer periods (see Diagram 184).

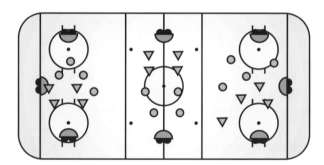

**Diagram 184**

Suitable play in both or one end zone is very popular way of improving the techniques learned. At the same time, other action can be taking place in the neutral zone. Here are some variations:

Play is with 3:3 in both end zones with the aim of man marking in defense. At the same time, other players can be carrying out the following exercises in the neutral zone:

- Playing a game of "Piggy in the middle" – the player in the center tries to intercept other players' passes.
- Playing "Piggy in the middle" in a circle – the player in the center of the circle tries to intercept the other players' passes. – after receiving the pass each player does a turn, goes down on one knee etc., only backhand passes are used, after receiving

the puck a long feinting maneuver is done, after receiving the puck with the stick it is played on using the skate.
- Improvement of individual puck handling (different variations of the feinting and dodging movements, passes, shots) or doing simple combinations (return passes in pairs, "give and go", crossing etc.).
- The next variation is done as 3:3 in one of the end zones. In the neutral zone, they play "Piggy in the middle" in a circle, and in the other end zone they work at improving individual puck handling. Another variation for 3:3 is where the passes may only be done on the backhand.

**Play in a confined space**

At an age of about 10 years, the players should learn to have a good, correct feeling for the playing area and cooperation with their teammates. For this, the most suitable games are those done in a confined space – close-quarters.

One variation often used is the game in the face-off circle. This can be done with different numbers of players, particularly in 1:1, 2:1, and 2:2 situations.

Playing 1:1 in each end zone. Two standing players assist the attacking player, who can pass the puck to them. A changeover takes place after 30 seconds (see Diagram 185).

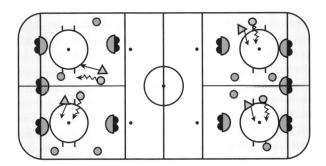

**Diagram 185**

A game 2:1 is played in each of the three areas:
- Crosswise, in one of the playing zones 2 x 2:1; the non-participating players are in the neutral zone.
- Playing 2:1 in the corner – the playing area is marked off – the other players stand behind the marked line (see Diagram 186).

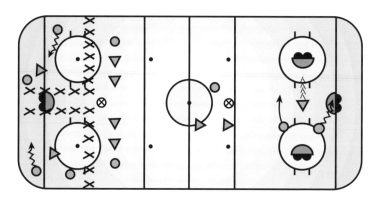

**Diagram 186**

Playing in the end zones 2:1 and 1:2. The zone is divided along its longest axis into two halves. The players may not go into the other half. They may only pass to their "own" teammate, who is in the second group in the other half (see Diagram 187).

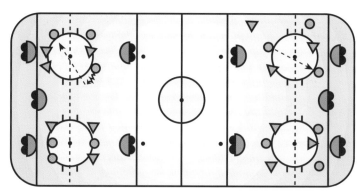

**Diagram 187**

Following on from this, games can be played with several goal mouths. The next diagram shows games 2:2, 3:3 against three goal mouths.

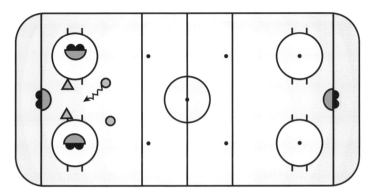

**Diagram 188**

The last example is a game with four goal mouths where they are turned backwards (see Diagram 189). The goals are turned round often in the individual zones for various different game variations. Play can be done with different numbers of players and several pucks in play at the same time.

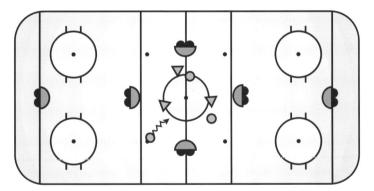

**Diagram 189**

For all these games (both in a playing zone as well as in a confined space) it is typical that they each has its own rules so that the trainer can manage them. This possibility is mainly used so that the technique being practiced is improved. Besides this, the young players have to find the best solution for each situation. In this way, the basics for cooperation and orientation on the ice is schooled into the young players.

# Training Examples – 9 Year Olds

| | | | |
|---|---|---|---|
| **Number:** | 5 | **Age Group:** | Nine year olds |
| **Date:** | August | **Number of players:** | 24 |
| **Total time:** | 60 minutes | **Number of trainers:** | 3 |
| **Location:** | Ice hockey Stadium | **Training aim:** | Skating, individual game techniques |

## Content of Training Unit

**Beginning:**
- Greeting, establishing positive motivation.
- Skating forwards with long glides on the outside edges.

**Warm-up and main part:**
- Doing cross-over steps forwards in a circle.
- Doing cross-over steps backwards in a circle.
- Doing cross-overs left, right in a snaking line (see Diagram 190).

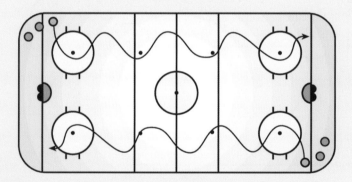

**Diagram 190**

- Leg stances: 1:1 in the zone, always crossing over to the left and the right.
- Puck handling in the zone, alternately short and long dribbling, shooting (see Diagram 191 a).
- Puck handling: Slalom doing little circles (see Diagram 191 b).

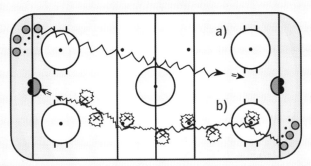

**Diagram 191**

- Game in individual playing zones 4:4 (see Diagram 192).

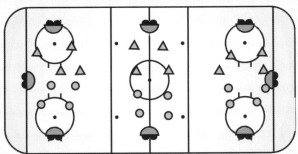

**Diagram 192**

**Conclusion:**
- Forehand wrist shots on the move.
- Stretching and breathing exercises.
- Meeting together – assessment of the training.

**Notes:**
- During the training session, include stretching and breathing exercises each time after an exercise.
- In between the individual exercises, time must be allowed to take a drink and to reorganize equipment.

| | | | |
|---|---|---|---|
| **Number:** | 10 | **Age Group:** | Nine year olds |
| **Date:** | August | **Number of players:** | 24 |
| **Total time:** | 75 minutes | **Number of trainers:** | 3 |
| **Location:** | Ice hockey Stadium | **Training aim:** | Skating, individual game techniques |

## Content of Training Unit

**Beginning:**

Greeting, motivation.

- Skating, keeping the legs parallel, not lifting up from the ice, doing a "ski slalom", skating tight and rapid circles alternating between larger and slower ones.
- Skating – cross-overs with glides on the outside edges.
- Short stretching exercises.

**Warm-up and main part:**

- Doing cross-over steps in a circle with a turn and a cross-over backwards (forwards), at a signal do a curve out of the circle backwards (forwards).
- Catching game 1:1: The follower skates forwards and the person being followed skates backwards. Tagging the head only counts as a catch.
- Puck handling when skating backwards with cross-overs in a circle.
- Puck handling with a quarter turn – forwards and backwards, shooting (see Diagram 193 a).
- Puck handling doing forwards/backwards cross-overs with turns (see Diagram 193 b).

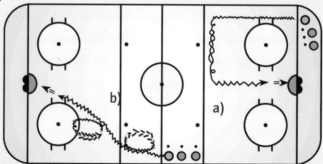

**Diagram 193**

- Game of 5:5: Using the whole ice and doing changes on the fly after 30-45 seconds.

## Conclusion:

■ Shooting practice: Skating backwards, receiving the puck, doing a quarter turn skating forwards followed by a shot.

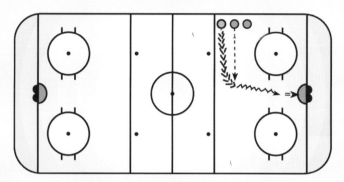

**Diagram 194**

■ Stretching and breathing exercises.
■ Meeting together – assessment of the training.

## Notes:

■ During the training session, include stretching and breathing exercises each time after an exercise.
■ Shorten the exercises where required, time must be allowed to take a drink and a timeout to reorganize equipment.

| | | | |
|---|---|---|---|
| **Number:** | 18 | **Age Group:** | Nine year olds |
| **Date:** | September | **Number of players:** | 40 |
| **Total time:** | 90 minutes | **Number of trainers:** | 5 |
| **Location:** | Ice hockey Stadium | **Training aim:** | Skating, individual game techniques, game |

## Content of Training Unit

**Beginning:**

- Greeting, motivation.
- A little game.
- Stretching.
- Skating with the puck, agility exercises.
- Starts without the puck from different positions – red goal line – blue defensive line 5 times, timeout between the repeats 1:10.
- The trainer gets the goalies to warm up.

**Warm-up and main part:**

- Working with 4 stations plus a station for goalies.
- Each change over after 10 minutes.
- After doing two stations repeat the start from different positions (from the blue line to the next blue line) 5 times, timeout 1:10.

**Stations:**

1. Cross-overs skating forwards, backwards – main emphasis is on the correct technique (Diagram 195 a).
2. In pairs – Passing and receiving the puck on the move (Diagram 195 b).
3. 2:1 – puck handling and passing (Diagram 195 c).
4. Skating forwards – long glides, correct technique (Diagram 195 d).
5. Goalie training – separate (Diagram 195 e).

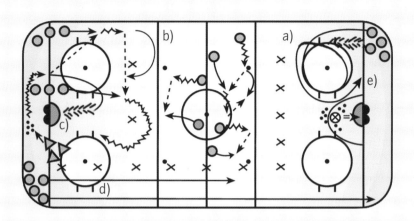

**Diagram 195**

- Game on the whole of the ice – 5:5 with changeover after 45-60 seconds.

## Conclusion:
- Little game without the sticks.
- Free skating without the puck – in groups led by the trainer.
- Stretching and breathing exercises.
- Meeting together – assessment of the training.

## Notes:
- During the training session, include stretching and breathing exercises each time after an exercise.
- In between the individual exercises, time must be allowed to take a drink and timeout to reorganize equipment.

| | | | |
|---|---|---|---|
| **Number:** | 36 | **Age Group:** | Nine year olds |
| **Date:** | October | **Number of players:** | 24 |
| **Total time:** | 75 minutes | **Number of trainers:** | 3 |
| **Location:** | Ice hockey Stadium | **Training aim:** | Skating, individual game techniques |

## Content of Training Unit

**Beginning:**

- Greeting, motivation.
- Catching game – "the Ram": The player being caught skates forwards, the other one skates backwards. The Ram can only touch the player being caught on the head, neither player may lift their legs off the ice.
- Stretching exercises.

**Warm-up and main part:**

- Ice-skating: Doing a cross-over forwards in a circle, the first half of the circle done as a glide, the second with a jump.
- Puck handling: Doing forwards cross-overs, alternating with full turns.

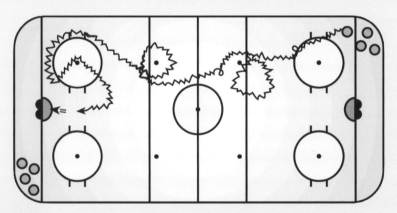

**Diagram 196**

- Passing in pairs: The first half is done sideways then facing each other – one player skates backwards.

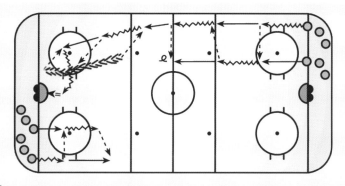

**Diagram 197**

- Game on the whole ice 5:5, changes on the fly after 30-45 seconds.

## Conclusion:

- Individual sprinting in the direction of the goal after having done two turns (two sets of people do the exercise at the same time at goals each end).

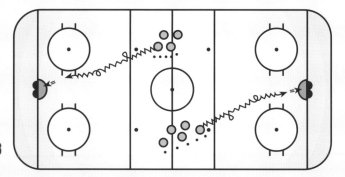

**Diagram 198**

- Stretching and breathing exercises.
- Meeting together – assessment of the training.

## Notes:

- During the training session, include stretching and breathing exercises each time after an exercise.
- Shorten the exercises where required, to allow time to take a drink and timeout to reorganize equipment.

| | | | |
|---|---|---|---|
| **Number:** | 56 | **Age Group:** | Nine year olds |
| **Date:** | December | **Number of players:** | 24 |
| **Total time:** | 75 minutes | **Number of trainers:** | 3 |
| **Location:** | Ice hockey Stadium | **Training aim:** | Skating, individual game techniques, game combinations |

## Content of Training Unit

**Beginning:**

- Greeting, motivation.
- Skating without the puck – long glides forwards, backwards.

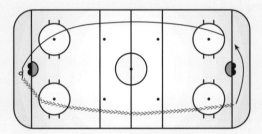

**Diagram 199**

- Stretching exercises.

**Warm-up and main part:**

- **Catching game 1:1:** Skate forwards, touch with the hand, the person being followed does as many turns as possible for which he gets points.
- **Ice-skating:** Doing cross-overs left-hand round a circle, on a signal do a flying turn to the right out of the circle.
- **Puck handling:** Do cross-overs forwards, carry out a complete turn and stop facing the center area of the ice, do cross-overs forwards and backwards, do cross-overs forwards – shoot.

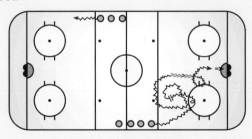

**Diagram 200**

- **Doing "drop pass" and back passes:** The players run along after each other, one behind the other. The player who does the drop pass executes a turn skating backwards and takes on a pass again.

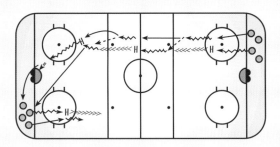

**Diagram 201**

- 1:1, the attacking player skates backwards and faces the puck as he takes the pass on.

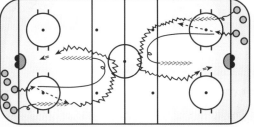

**Diagram 202**

- Controlled game: 5:5 on the whole of the ice.

**Conclusion:**
- Puck handling: Pulling the puck on to the stick and individually skating at goal.
- Stretching and breathing exercises.
- Meeting together – assessment of the training.

**Notes:**
- During the training session, include stretching and breathing exercises each time after an exercise.
- Shorten the exercises where required, to allow a timeout to take a drink and to reorganize equipment between the individual exercises.

| | | | |
|---|---|---|---|
| **Number:** | 61 | **Age Group:** | Nine year olds |
| **Date:** | December | **Number of players:** | 40 |
| **Total time:** | 90 minutes | **Number of trainers:** | 5 |
| **Location:** | Ice hockey Stadium | **Training aim:** | Skating, individual game techniques |

## Content of Training Unit

**Beginning:**

- Greeting, positive motivation.
- Free skating in groups with stretching exercises.
- Shooting practice – at both goals, any speed, on a signal the players skate from the neutral zone and finish off with a shot at either goal. After the shot they take the puck back into the neutral zone. The main emphasis lies on agility exercises before taking the shot (kneeling down on one leg, turning, rolling over etc.).

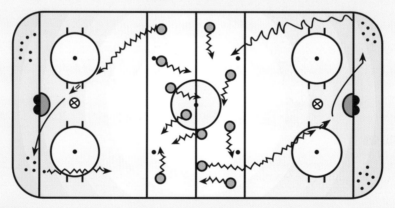

**Diagram 203**

- Starts without the puck from different positions (10-15 m), five repeats with timeouts 1:10.

**Warm-up and main part:**

- Exercises at 5 stations: Change round after 10 minutes. A trainer or one of his assistants is at each station.

**Stations:**

**1)** Skate forwards, skate backwards, puck handling and shooting twice. The trainer plays the puck back into the center.

**2)** Puck handling while doing a slalom skating forwards – the stick leads the puck on the leg side, back to puck handling skating backwards.

**3)** Puck handling while doing a slalom skating forwards – the stick leads the puck on the other side, back to puck handling skating backwards.

**4)** Puck handling, ducking under hurdles, doing shots. The trainer feeds the player with a fresh puck as he skates backwards.

**5)** Puck handling – pass off the boards, jump over hurdles (twice), pass off the boards, skate round a cone, skate backwards, skate forwards and do a shot. The trainer feeds the player a fresh puck as he skates backwards.

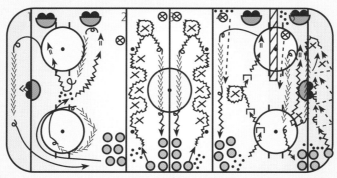

**Diagram 204**

■ Controlled game 5:5, regular changeovers after 40-50 seconds.

**Conclusion:**
■ Little games without a stick.
■ Stretching and breathing exercises.
■ Meeting together – assessment of the training.

**Notes:**
■ During the training session, include stretching and breathing exercises each time after an exercise.
■ Shorten the exercises where required, to allow a timeout to take a drink and to reorganize equipment between the individual exercises.

| Number: | 82 | Age Group: | Nine year olds |
|---|---|---|---|
| Date: | February | Number of players: | 40 |
| Total time: | 90 minutes | Number of trainers: | 5 |
| Location: | Ice hockey Stadium | Training aim: | Skating, individual game techniques, game combinations |

## Content of Training Unit

**Beginning:**

- Greeting, motivation.
- Free skating with the puck, agility exercises. Each trainer is with his group.
- Stretching exercises.
- Shooting practice – the players without a puck skate forwards, backwards doing agility exercises, at the blue line they receive the puck and shoot at the goalie (using only the wrist shot) – see Diagram 205. Play is at any speed with a shot at either goal.

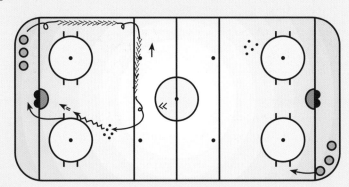

**Diagram 205**

- Starts without the puck from different positions – from between the one blue line to the other blue line, five repeats with timeouts 1:10.

**Warm-up and main part:**

- Exercises at 4 stations: Change round after every 10-15 minutes. A trainer or one of his assistants is at each station.

**Stations:**

**1)** Puck handling down a slalom doing a dodging movement against the trainer then shoot.

**2)** Skating backwards, receive a pass, play round the trainer then shoot.

**3)** Ice-skating – correct technique, all do one exercise together and the move on to the next exercise (skate a tight curve, turning the defender, skating round cones, curves with cross-overs)

**4)** 2:1 situation – main emphasis – passing and correct movements of the defending players (skating at them and keeping close contact).

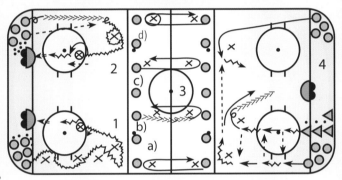

**Diagram 206**

■ Controlled game 5:5, explanation of the players positions in the defending zone from the viewpoint of the positioning and area (two defenders, one player pulled back, two forwards).

**Conclusion:**
■ Shooting competition – the players must do an agility exercise before the shot.
■ Stretching and breathing exercises.
■ Meeting together – assessment of the training.

**Notes:**
■ During the training session, include stretching and breathing exercises each time after an exercise.
■ Shorten the exercises where required, to allow a timeout to take a drink and to reorganize equipment between the individual exercises.

| | | | |
|---|---|---|---|
| **Number:** | 96 | **Age Group:** | Nine year olds |
| **Date:** | March | **Number of players:** | 24 |
| **Total time:** | 75 minutes | **Number of trainers:** | 3 |
| **Location:** | Ice hockey Stadium | **Training aim:** | Skating, individual game techniques |

## Content of Training Unit

**Beginning:**

- Greeting, positive motivation.
- Skating forwards with cross-overs, skate backwards doing half turns

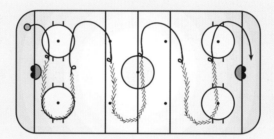

**Diagram 207**

- Little games without a stick.
- Stretching exercises.

**Warm-up and main part:**

- Stopping on the left side – doing a half-turn to the left – doing a complete turn to the right – stopping on the right side – doing a half-turn to the right.

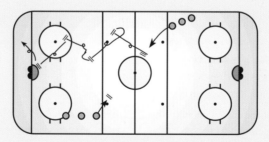

**Diagram 208**

- **Puck handling with cross-overs – left-handers:** After doing a flying half-turn to the left, pull the puck to the stick, change then do a flying half-turn and a dodge to one side. Right-handers vice versa.

- **Puck handling:** Do cross-overs forwards, backwards, pass off the boards, receive the puck on the turn, do a feint and dodge against a cone, do a three-quarter turn then shoot.

**Diagram 209**

- **1:1 situation:** Start from the blue line in the neutral zone , the defending player dribbles the puck and passes off the boards to the right, the attacking player receives the puck on the turn, leads it off diagonally to the other side, does a rebound pass off the boards to himself, gathers the puck up on the turn and concludes the movement. The second player continues skating forward, defending in the neutral zone after having given up the pass.

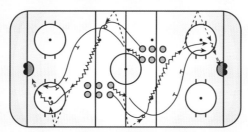

**Diagram 210**

- **Controlled game 5:5:** Play over the whole of the ice in the basic layout 2-1-2 in the defending zone.

**Conclusion:**
- Shots with crossing of the legs.
- Stretching and breathing exercises.
- Meeting together – assessment of the training.

**Notes:**
- During the training session, include stretching and breathing exercises each time after an exercise.
- Shorten the exercises where required, to allow a timeout to take a drink and to reorganize equipment between the individual exercises.

# Training Examples – 10 Year Olds

| | | | |
|---|---|---|---|
| **Number:** | 2 | **Age Group:** | Ten year olds |
| **Date:** | August | **Number of players:** | 24 |
| **Total time:** | 60 minutes | **Number of trainers:** | 3 |
| **Location:** | Ice hockey Stadium | **Training aim:** | Skating, individual game techniques |

## Content of Training Unit

**Beginning:**
- Greeting, positive motivation.
- Skating round the ice with long glides on the outside edges.

**Warm-up and main part:**
- Doing cross-over steps forwards – left, right in snaking lines with flying turns in the curves.

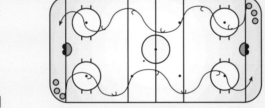

**Diagram 211**

- Doing cross-over steps backwards – left, right in snaking lines with flying turns in the curves.
- **Puck handling:** Short and long dribbling alternately, pulling the puck in onto the stick and doing a long dodging movement to one side with cross-overs to the right, left in a snaking line then shoot.

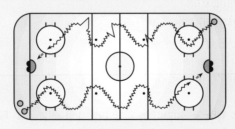

**Diagram 212**

- **Puck handling:** Forwards, backwards, passes off the boards finishing with a shot at goal.

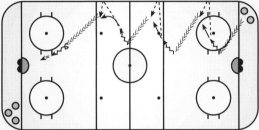

**Diagram 213**

- **Game in a playing zones 2 x 3:3:** The other players play the game of "Piggy in the middle" in the neutral zone. After receiving the puck, the player has to do a long dodging movement to one side.

## Conclusion:

- Puck handling, finishing off with a shot.

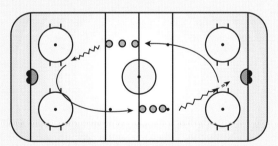

**Diagram 214**

- Stretching and breathing exercises.
- Meeting together – assessment of the training.

## Notes:

- During the training session, include stretching and breathing exercises each time after an exercise.
- Shorten the exercises where required, to allow a timeout to take a drink and to reorganize equipment between the individual exercises.

| Number: | 5 | Age Group: | Ten year olds |
|---|---|---|---|
| Date: | August | Number of players: | 26 |
| Total time: | 60 minutes | Number of trainers: | 3 |
| Location: | Ice hockey Stadium | Training aim: | Skating, individual game techniques |

## Content of Training Unit

**Beginning:**

- Greeting, positive motivation, content of the training session.
- Puck handling round the ice, any speed, doing various dribbling methods.
- Stretching exercises.

**Warm-up and main part:**

- **Puck handling:** Each of five players skates round the cones, forwards, backwards, alternately forwards and backwards, doing turns. In the second goal the goalie is warming up.

**Diagram 215**

- **Puck handling:** Doing a turn by the cones, shooting, carry on behind the goal net, turn to skate backwards, forwards – join the other group.

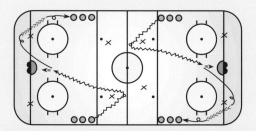

**Diagram 216**

- **Shooting on the move after a pass:** On a signal at the same time from both sides, after delivering the shot skate behind the cone and then skate forwards with 2 turns (left and right).

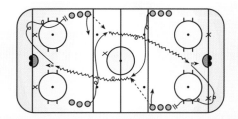

**Diagram 217**

- **1:1:** The defender plays in the puck. After the conclusion both players skate round the cones.

**Diagram 218**

- Group training (the players are changed over once)
- **a)** Mini hockey in one of the playing zones 4:4 (5:5).
- **b)** Shooting off the boards (perfecting the method).
- **c)** Passing – in pairs on the spot.

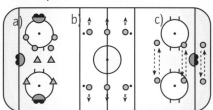

**Diagram 219**

**Conclusion:**
- Free skating without the puck, forwards, backwards.
- Stretching and breathing exercises.
- Meeting together – assessment of the training.

**Notes:**
- During the training session, include stretching and breathing exercises each time after an exercise.
- Shorten the exercises where required, to allow a timeout to take a drink and to reorganize equipment between the individual exercises.

| Number: | 14 | Age Group: | Ten year olds |
|---|---|---|---|
| Date: | August | Number of players: | 24 |
| Total time: | 75 minutes | Number of trainers: | 3 |
| Location: | Ice hockey Stadium | Training aim: | Skating, individual game techniques |

## Content of Training Unit

**Beginning:**
- Greeting, positive motivation.
- Game "all against all". Who keeps possession of the puck the longest and who scores a goal?

**Warm-up and main part:**
- Skating without a puck around a marked off course, skating alternately forwards and backwards, change direction each time at the middle of the curve.

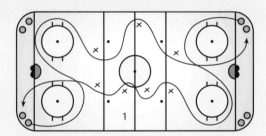

**Diagram 220**

- **Puck handling:** Agility exercises, shooting at goal.

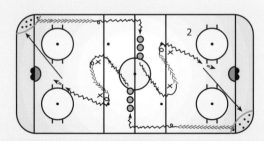

**Diagram 221**

- **Shooting at the goalie:** In pairs, the player without the puck follows on behind the player with the puck as fast as possible. Six repeats (one player three times as the leader and three times as the second man).

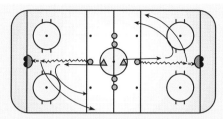

**Diagram 222**

■ **Passing:** 2:0, on both sides at the same time, start on a whistle.

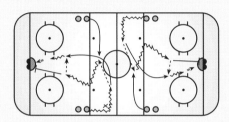

**Diagram 223**

■ **1:1:** The attacking player starts off with the puck in the center circle, the defender defends on the other side. The exercise takes place on both sides of the ice at the same time (start with a whistle). The players change over defending and attacking roles.

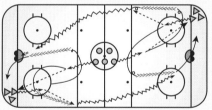

**Diagram 224**

■ Game of mini hockey in individual playing zones 4:4.

**Conclusion:**

■ Free skating in groups with the trainer.
■ Stretching and breathing exercises.
■ Meeting together – assessment of the training.

**Notes:**

■ During the training session, include stretching and breathing exercises each time after an exercise.
■ Shorten the exercises where required, to allow a timeout to take a drink and to reorganize equipment between the individual exercises.

| | | | |
|---|---|---|---|
| **Number:** | 26 | **Age Group:** | Ten year olds |
| **Date:** | September | **Number of players:** | 24 |
| **Total time:** | 60 minutes | **Number of trainers:** | 3 |
| **Location:** | Ice hockey Stadium | **Training aim:** | Skating, individual game techniques |

## Content of Training Unit

**Beginning:**

- Greeting, positive motivation.
- Skating backwards, turn into cross-overs forwards.

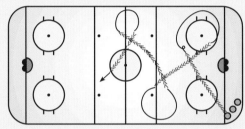

**Diagram 225**

- Stretching exercises.

**Warm-up and main part:**

- Doing cross-over steps left round a circle, flying right-handed turn and straight away whole turn round to the left.
- **Puck handling:** Cross-overs left, right, pulling the puck in onto the stick and doing a long dodging movement to one side with cross-overs to the right, when doing cross-overs change over.

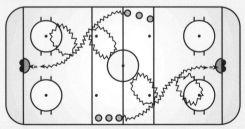

**Diagram 226**

- **Puck handling + 1:1:** The attacking player receives the puck in the center circle, in the end zone he changes over to skate backwards and then back again skating forwards. He then skates into the neutral zone and back into the attacking zone

228

into a 1:1 situation. The defending player starts by skating backwards, on the centerline he turns to skate forwards, does a tight curve in the end zone and skates back into the neutral zone. With a braked curve stop, he comes skating backwards and defends in the 1:1 situation. The defenders and attackers change over roles.

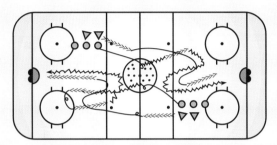

**Diagram 227**

- **Game 2:1:** Play is in three places at the same time:
- **a)** Crosswise in one of the zones 2 x 2:1, the non-playing participant waits in the neutral zone.
- **b)** In the corners: The playing area is marked off, the non-playing participant stands behind the marked-off area.

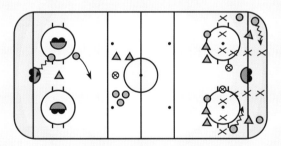

**Diagram 228**

## Conclusion:

- Shooting on the backhand.
- Stretching and breathing exercises.
- Meeting together – assessment of the training.

## Notes:

- During the training session, include stretching and breathing exercises each time after an exercise.
- Shorten the exercises where required, to allow a timeout to take a drink and to reorganize equipment between the individual exercises.

| | | | |
|---|---|---|---|
| **Number:** | 40 | **Age Group:** | Ten year olds |
| **Date:** | October | **Number of players:** | 24 |
| **Total time:** | 75 minutes | **Number of trainers:** | 3 |
| **Location:** | Ice hockey Stadium | **Training aim:** | Skating, individual game techniques, game combinations |

## Content of Training Unit

**Beginning:**

- Greeting, positive motivation.
- Skating round the ice with long curves and cross-overs, skate diagonally through the zone in curves on one skate.

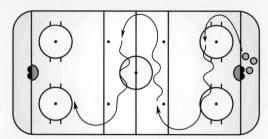

**Diagram 229**

- Stretching exercises

**Warm-up and main part:**

- Doing cross-over steps round a circle – quick turns to the left, right.
- **Catching game 1:1:** The follower gains points for a flying turn and kneeling down.
- **Puck handling:** Do a slalom course, various dodging maneuvers with feints, dodging into the opposite direction, also before doing a shot at goal.

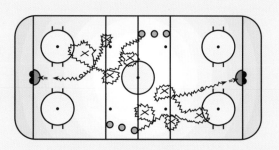

**Diagram 230**

- **Puck handling:** Pass, drop pass, crossing and then further as in Diagram 231.

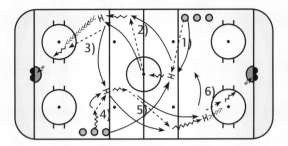

**Diagram 231**

- **Crossing:** Pass, tackling a man in attacking zone, in the neutral zone 1:1 situation facing each other.

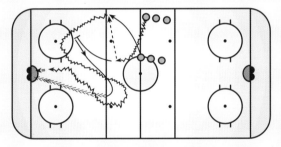

**Diagram 232**

- **Game 5:5:** On the whole of the ice, free play, changing on the fly after 40 seconds.

## Conclusion:
- Individual starts from the blue line 'running' on the tips of the skates, pulling the puck in onto the stick and doing a dodging maneuver to one side.
- Stretching and breathing exercises.
- Meeting together – assessment of the training.

## Notes:
- During the training session, include stretching and breathing exercises each time after an exercise.
- Shorten the exercises where required, to allow a timeout to take a drink and to reorganize equipment between the individual exercises.

| | | | |
|---|---|---|---|
| **Number:** | 65 | **Age Group:** | Ten year olds |
| **Date:** | December | **Number of players:** | 24 |
| **Total time:** | 75 minutes | **Number of trainers:** | 7 |
| **Location:** | Ice hockey Stadium | **Training aim:** | Coordination exercises, individual game techniques |

## Content of Training Unit

**Beginning:**

- Greeting, positive motivation.
- Ice-skating – on one side gymnastic swinging exercises, on the other side ice-skating forwards, backwards, turns, skating curves on the edges of the skates, skating on one leg etc.
- Little games.
- Static stretching exercises.

**Warm-up and main part:**

- **Doing short passes:** Four groups of players. The goalie is warming up with the trainer.

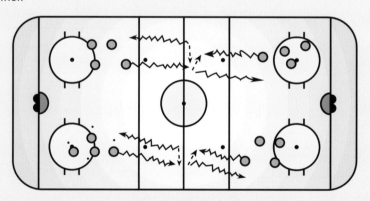

**Diagram 233**

- **Puck handling and passing:** The player passes the puck off and at the same time he receives a puck pass from the other direction from the trainer. The exercise takes place on only one side of the ice, on the other side the puck is moved about freely – dodging maneuvers, feinting, turns, wrist shots.

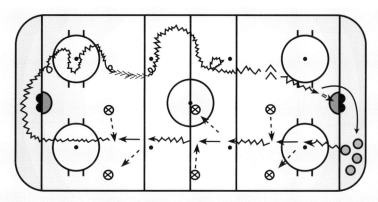

**Diagram 234**

■ **Puck exchanging – shooting:** The players start at the same time on a whistle. The exercise takes place on both sides of the ice at the same time, the players from groups A & D start together and the players from groups B & C wait (with a changeover after a particular time), puck exchanges, shots at goal.

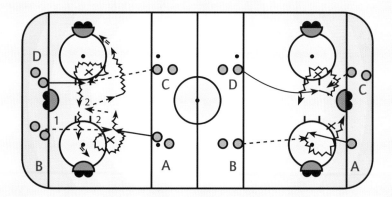

**Diagram 235**

■ **Team competition:** Each player starts 4 times, timeouts 1:8 (development of speed).

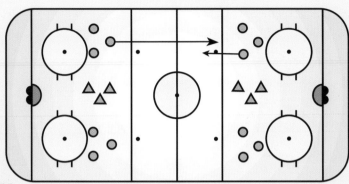

**Diagram 236**

■ **Shooting 1:1:** The exercise takes place in both halves of the ice at the same time. The player starts from the center circle of the ice, skating backwards without the puck, he then receives the puck from a pass and turns into skating forwards, plays the puck passing it to the other player on the goal crease line. He then skates on with the puck. The first player skates backwards further to the boards, receives a pass and brings it into the neutral zone, passes it into the center, does a turn into skating backwards and comes onto the boards, receives a pass back and shoots from the edge of the circle and reaches the goal line. The player skates from the goal line into the center circle again. Done alternately from the right and the left.

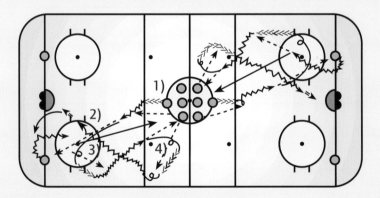

**Diagram 237**

■ **Controlled exercises:** These take place in both halves of the ice with 4 groups each with a puck. The player skates without the puck, does a turn to skate backwards, receives a pass, skates round the cones, passes the puck into the other corner, turns round and receives the puck back from his group. After receiving the pass he shoots straight away at goal. Just before he shoots, the trainer tells him where he is to shoot.

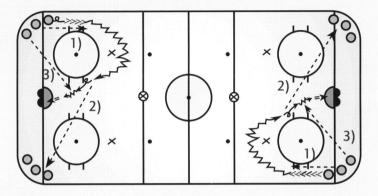

**Diagram 238**

■ Free game 5:5 on the whole of the ice, change on the fly after 40 seconds.

## Conclusion:

■ Individual starts from the blue line, takes place on both sides, shortly before shooting kneel down and then do a turn.
■ Stretching and breathing exercises.
■ Meeting together – assessment of the training.

## Notes:

■ During the training session, include stretching and breathing exercises each time after an exercise.
■ Shorten the exercises where required, to allow a timeout to take a drink and to reorganize equipment between the individual exercises.

| | | | |
|---|---|---|---|
| **Number:** | 86 | **Age Group:** | Ten year olds |
| **Date:** | January | **Number of players:** | 30 |
| **Total time:** | 90 minutes | **Number of trainers:** | 5 |
| **Location:** | Ice hockey Stadium | **Training aim:** | Skating, individual game techniques |

## Content of Training Unit

**Beginning:**
- Greeting, positive motivation.
- Skating without the puck.
- Game "each against the other".
- Stretching exercises.

**Warm-up and main part:**
- Exercise in five stations. Change round each time after 12 minutes. A trainer or his assistant is at each station.

**Stations:**

**1)** 1:1: The defender on the blue line passes the puck to the attacking player, then he comes in between the cones, receives the second puck from the corner, shoots at goal, turns round to skate backwards and defends himself in a 1:1 situation facing the opponent, change of position.

**2)** Shooting – onto the boards, different variations.

**3)** 1:1: Agility skating exercises, on the blue line turning into a 1:1 situation.

**4)** Man marking 1:1 – in a marked-off area.

**5)** 2:0 + 1:1: Emphasis is on passing play and receiving the puck. The players change over in defense.

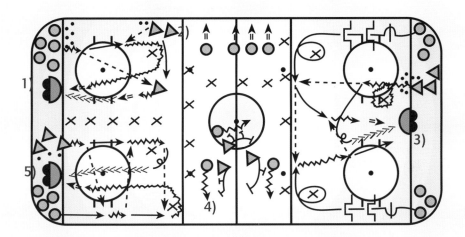

**Diagram 239**

- **Game 5:5:** Takes place over the whole ice. Change round after 40 seconds, emphasis – 1:1 situations.

## Conclusion:

- Individual starts with agility exercises prior to doing a shot at goal.
- Stretching and breathing exercises.
- Meeting together – assessment of the training.

## Notes:

- During the training session, include stretching and breathing exercises each time after an exercise.
- Shorten the exercises where required, to allow a timeout to take a drink and to reorganize equipment between the individual exercises.

| | | | |
|---|---|---|---|
| **Number:** | **92** | **Age Group:** | Ten year olds |
| **Date:** | February | **Number of players:** | 24 |
| **Total time:** | 75 minutes | **Number of trainers:** | 3 |
| **Location:** | Ice hockey Stadium | **Training aim:** | Skating, individual game techniques, game combinations |

## Content of Training Unit

**Beginning:**

■ Greeting, positive motivation.

■ Skating, curves on the outside edge of the inside-leg skate.

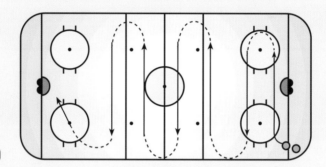

**Diagram 240**

■ Stretching exercises.

**Warm-up and main part:**

■ Ice-skating, curves right and left, when changing direction keep the legs further apart and do cross-overs.

■ Puck handling round the face-off circle to the right, do a flying turn to the left (outwards), turn right etc.

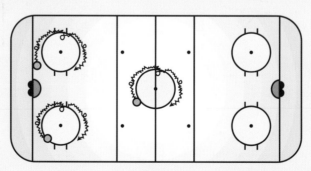

**Diagram 241**

■ **Puck handling:** Do a flying turn when doing a cross-over – dodging maneuver – flying turn – pull the puck onto the stick – flying turn – hand feint – etc – changeover.

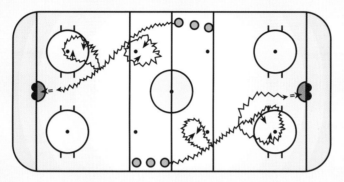

**Diagram 242**

■ 2:0 with a drop pass and transition to a 1:1 situation. Two couples start at the same time, exchange puck passes twice, in the neutral zone the players with the puck pass to the player without the puck in the opposite direction. They take the puck on and do a drop pass to the player. This player leads the puck in the direction of the goal, turns into skating backwards and passes the puck to a teammate with whom he started the action and defends in a 1:1 situation. All the players start on a signal.

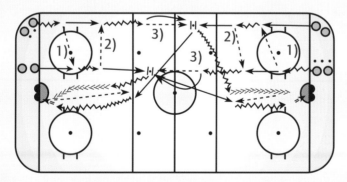

**Diagram 243**

■ **Game 1:1:** Takes place in the end zones in both halves of the ice, each attacking player has two persons assisting (he can pass the puck to them). Changeover of players after 30 seconds.

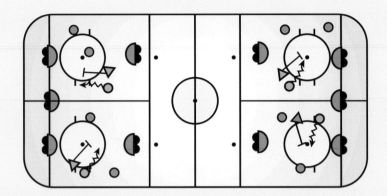

**Diagram 244**

- **Free play 5:5:** On the whole of the ice, change on the fly after 40 seconds.

## Conclusion:

- Individual starts in the direction of the goalie after a whole turn while kneeling (dribbling also while kneeling).

- Stretching and breathing exercises.

- Meeting together – assessment of the training.

## Notes:

- During the training session, include stretching and breathing exercises each time after an exercise.

- Shorten the exercises where required, to allow a timeout to take a drink and to reorganize equipment between the individual exercises.

| | | | |
|---|---|---|---|
| **Number:** | 110 | **Age Group:** | Ten year olds |
| **Date:** | March | **Number of players:** | 24 |
| **Total time:** | 75 minutes | **Number of trainers:** | 3 |
| **Location:** | Ice hockey Stadium | **Training aim:** | Skating, individual game techniques, game combinations |

## Content of Training Unit

**Beginning:**

- Greeting, positive motivation.
- Individual free warming up on the ice using those skills already learned.
- Stretching exercises.

**Warm-up and main part:**

- **Puck handling skating the snake:** Use the skating skills learned, pull the puck on to the stick and dodge to the side, conclude with a shot at goal.

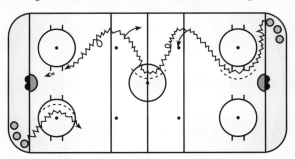

**Diagram 245**

- **Puck handling:** Do drop passes to each other, feinting and dodging, conclude with a shot at goal.

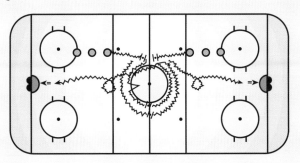

**Diagram 246**

- **Return passing:** The player from group A starts off with the puck in the neutral zone and skates towards the other blue line, exchanges the puck with the player from group B, who has also started off with a puck. Player A skates backwards, makes a puck exchange skates forwards and does a drop pass to Player B while skating backwards. He turns into skating forwards and concludes with a shot at goal. Player B then skates over to the other side etc.

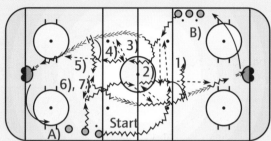

**Diagram 247**

- **Game in the end zones 2:1 (1:2):** The players may not leave their half of the ice, they can only pass the puck to their own teammate.

**Diagram 248**

- **Game 5:5 on the whole of the ice**, change on the fly after 40 seconds.

**Conclusion:**
- Individual starts after doing different variations of dodging and feinting maneuvers.
- Stretching and breathing exercises.
- Meeting together – assessment of the training.

**Notes:**
- During the training session, include stretching and breathing exercises each time after an exercise.
- Shorten the exercises where required, to allow a timeout to take a drink and to reorganize equipment between the individual exercises.

# 16 Exercises

## 16.1 Individual Game Play

### Exercise 1
**Ice-skating:**
- **a)** Changing over from skating backwards to skating forwards.
- **b)** Doing cross-overs when skating forwards, jumping over objects.
- **c)** Doing cross-overs when skating backwards.

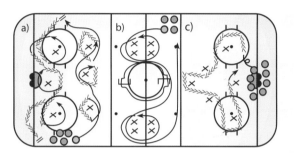

### Exercise 2
Puck handling, doing a turn by the cone, shot at goal, skate forwards, at the cone turn into skating backwards.

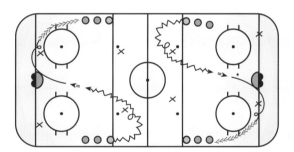

### Exercise 3
Passing when skating forwards, receiving a pass when skating backwards with changeovers into skating forwards.

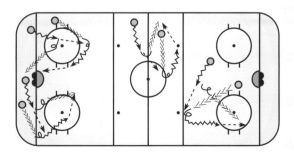

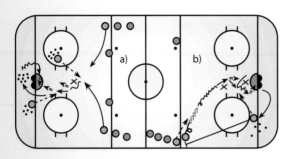

## Exercise 4

1:0:

**a)** After the pass, two shots at goal, conclude after skating round behind the goal net.

**b)** 2 shots at goal after doing a dodging maneuver.

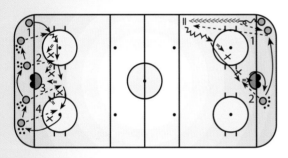

## Exercise 5

1:0:

**a)** 4 shots at goal after receiving a pass.

**b)** Shots at goal, finish off in front of the goal after a pass.

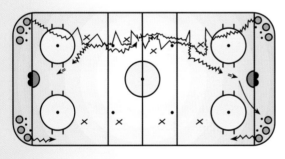

## Exercise 6

1:0, puck handling against each other at the same time, feinting, dodging, drop pass in the marked-off area, goal shot.

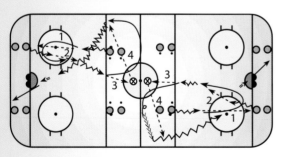

## Exercise 7

1:0, shooting at goal on the move. Four groups of players in one half of the ice – on both halves on a whistle signal at the same time.

## Exercise 8

**1:0, shooting practice:**

**a)** The player plays the puck on and follows it.

**b)** After doing the pass, carry out puck handling, jumps over a hurdle – rapid shot at goal, jumps over a second hurdle and does another shot at goal after receiving a pass.

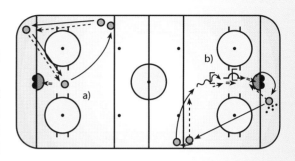

## Exercise 9

1:0, repeat goal shots three times – one after the other. The player skates on and turns to skate backwards (continuing as in the Diagram).

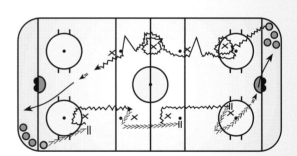

## Exercise 10

1:0, puck handling skating forwards and backwards round the cones, dodging maneuvers, feinting and shots at goal.

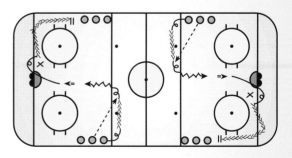

## Exercise 11

1:0, shots at goal, the player skates forwards, turns to skate backwards, receives the puck and shoots at goal, after shooting he increases speed, skates round the cone and continues by skating backwards.

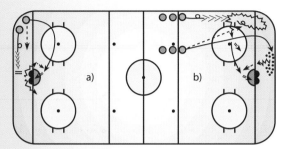

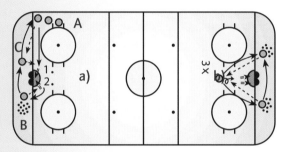

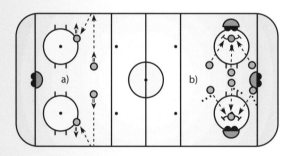

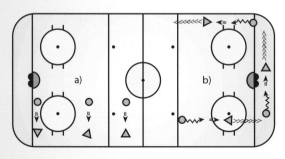

### Exercise 12
**1:0, shooting after receiving a pass:**

**a)** The player comes in skating from the corner, turns to skate backwards and passes the puck in front of the goal.

**b)** The player skates off from the blue line, turns to skate backwards and then back to skate forwards and then continues as in the Diagram. He shoots twice at goal.

### Exercise 13
**1:0:**

**a)** The player comes in skating from the corner and after receiving a pass; he shoots twice at goal. The order of players is from A to B, from B to C, from C to A.

**b)** The player in front of the goal shoots after doing a turn and receiving two passes (altogether he shoots 6 pucks, after this the players change over).

### Exercise 14

**a)** Follow-up shots; the player who shoots the follow-up shot is standing with his back to the shooter.

**b)** Feinting, using screening and doing follow-up shots.

### Exercise 15
**Different variation sets to block shots:**

**a)** From a standing position.

**b)** On the move.

**Exercise 16**
Stopping the puck.

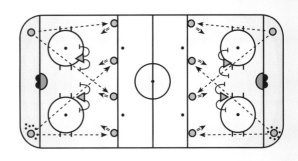

**Exercise 17**
**a)** Skating without the puck, emphasis – speed and agility, regeneration 1:8.
**b)** Shots at goal – the player starts off with the puck, plays the puck off the boards back to himself, turns to skate backwards, returns round the cone, does goal shots, the player joins the other group.

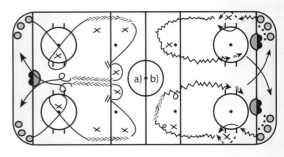

**Exercise 18**
1:0, Shooting after receiving a pass:
**a)** Following the puck.
**b)** Puck handling, doing goal shots after receiving a pass.

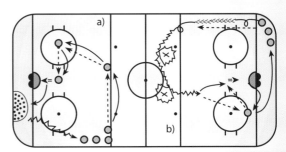

**Exercise 19**
1:0, shots at goal after receiving a pass and doing agility exercises.

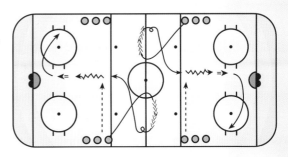

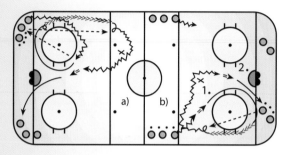

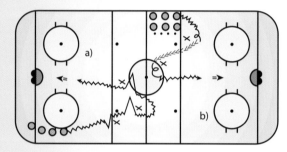

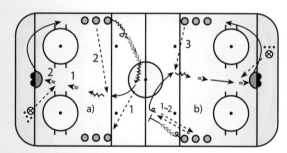

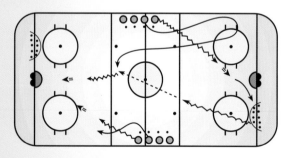

## Exercise 20

1:0:

**a)** The player with the puck skates round the circle, does a back pass, skates backwards, receives a puck pass, does a wrist shot.

**b)** The player starts off with the puck from the blue line and shoots at goal, skates backwards round the circle, receives a second puck pass and shoots behind the cone.

## Exercise 21

1:0:

**a)** Puck handling, dodging maneuvers in the opposite direction away from the cone, wrist shot.

**b)** Puck handling, skate forwards and backwards, wrist shot.

## Exercise 22

1:0 – double goal shots:

**a)** The player starts off with the puck, passes to the second group, receives the second puck from his own group and shoots at goal, after a pass in from the trainer followed up by a second shot at goal.

**b)** Skating backwards, the player with the puck exchanges the puck with another player from the group, in front of the blue line he receives a puck from the other side and shoots twice at goal.

## Exercise 23

Timing – basic exercise. After doing the shot, the player fetches the puck and passes it to another player. He follows the dotted line with his movements.

248

## Exercise 24

### Timing – similar exercise:

**a)** Skate forwards in a curve from the face-off circle, pass.

**b)** Skate forwards in a curve from the boards towards the face-off circle, pass.

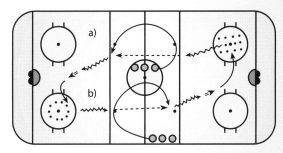

## Exercise 25

Timing. The player with the puck skates round the cone and passes the puck to another player, who has to time his movements.

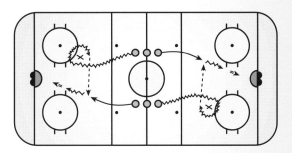

## Exercise 26

Timing. Preparatory exercise for a quick attack.

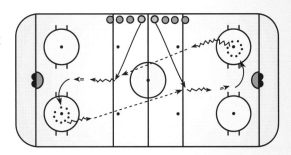

## Exercise 27

Timing. The player with the puck starts off from the boards, passes to another player in the corner and skates further on down the dotted line. The player in the corner matches his movements so that he can pass the puck to the player in position towards the blue line.

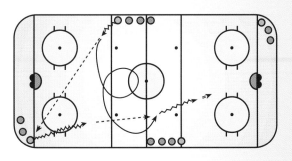

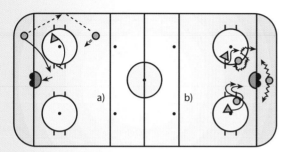

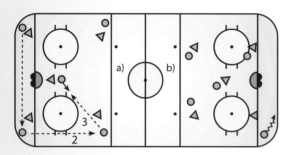

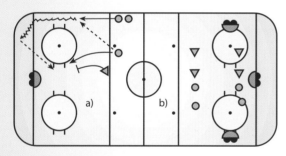

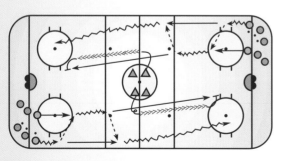

## Exercise 28

Breaking out free and covering the player without the puck:

**a]** The attacking player breaks free in front of the goal to do a feint and follows up with a shot. The defending player marks the player without the puck.

**b]** The attacking players part short of the goal in order to do a shot. The defending player marks them.

## Exercise 29

**a]** Do three passes without any opposition present, they are only covering, after the third pass, the defense becomes active 1:1.

**b]** The defending players hold their sticks reversed.

## Exercise 30

**a]** Covering and breaking free by the player without the puck.

**b]** Covering and breaking out free.

## Exercise 31

Covering of the player without the puck. The player with the puck in the attacking zone has to pass to his teammate, who breaks out free.

## Exercise 32

Backchecking. The backchecking player prevents the forward from being able to receive a pass from the center. In the exercise, roles and sides are changed round.

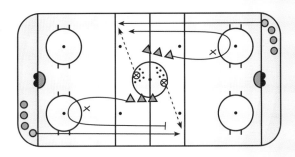

## Exercise 33

Backchecking of the player with the puck. The backchecking player tries to get in front of the forward to prevent a shot at goal. In the exercise, roles and sides are changed round.

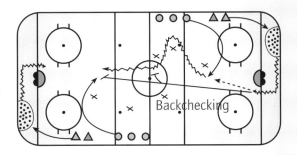

## Exercise 34

Covering the player without the puck in the defending zone. The defending player covers and marks the forward without the puck while skating backwards.

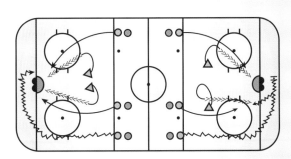

## Exercise 35

Checking in the attacking zone – preparatory exercise. Skating in a curve, skating up to the opponent and pushing him away from the central axis are all important for this. Return also skating in a curve.

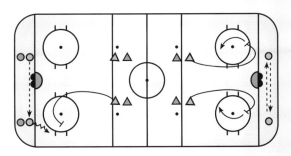

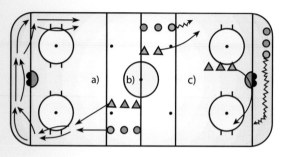

### Exercise 36

**a)** Checking – making contact (without the puck).

**b)** Checking the player with the puck along the boards – get in front of the forward with the shoulder. Constant control of the opponent's stick and his body.

**c)** Checking, the opponent skates behind the goal net.

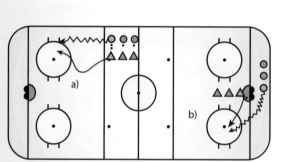

### Exercise 37

Checking and gaining possession of the puck by using the stick lifting method. Here, it is important to start properly, the defender has to get in front of the opponent, place his stick under the opponent's and maintain the same skating speed.

**a)** On the boards.

**b)** In clear areas.

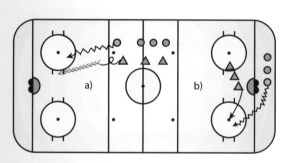

### Exercise 38

Checking the opponent with the puck and gaining possession of the puck by hooking out – the player with the puck should let the defender manage to do this and carry out his defense. It is important, not to hold the stick too far away from the body and to hook the puck out forward at the suitable moment by making a quick movement of the arms and the stick.

**a)** The defender skates backwards.

**b)** The defender skates forwards.

## Exercise 39

Checking the player by closing contact with him – the defending player starts off at the moment when the forward is behind the line, the forward can stop abruptly or change skating direction, the defending player should make proper contact and push the opponent towards the boards.

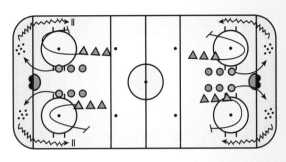

## Exercise 40

### Tackling techniques:

**a)** The defending player covers the puck (either facing or with his back to the opponent).

**b)** In the corner.

**c)** The puck is between the players (start with a whistle signal).

**d)** The players are at right-angles to each other and start off towards the puck.

**e)** The puck is in the circle – zone defense.

**f)** Three players – one player defends the player with the puck, who remains still.

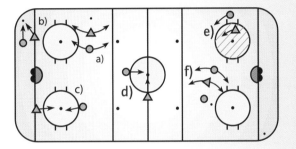

## Exercise 41

The basic exercise for the correct defending player's position – between the puck and his own goal (defensive positioning) – exercised also without a puck.

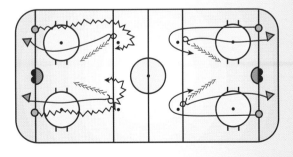

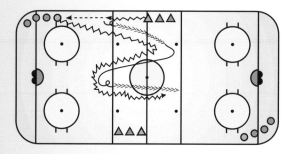

### Exercise 42

Man marking – the defending player alternates between skating forwards and backwards and keeps only a short distance away from the opponent. The exercise is done on both sides of the ice at the same time.

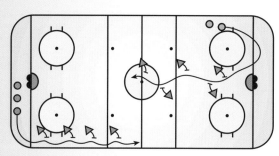

### Exercise 43

Preparatory exercises for tackling (hard) – without and with the puck, the defending player without a stick and also with a reversed stick.

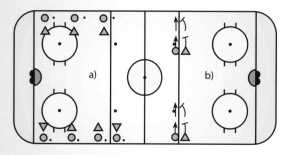

### Exercise 44
**Tackling:**

**a)** On the boards – the player with the puck is facing or with his back to the boards.

**b)** In an area – with and without the puck, the defending player without a stick, with a reversed stick, emphasis is on the correct technique.

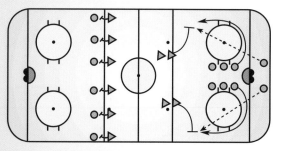

### Exercise 45

**a)** Preparation for tackling – different variations of pushing the opponent away (with the shoulder, chest, the hips etc.,) standing and on the move.

**b)** Checking and tackling on the boards.

**Exercise 46**

Backchecking leading up to a 1:1 situation. The trainer passes the puck to the forward in different positions on the ice.

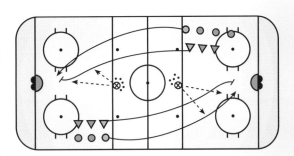

**Exercise 47**

**a)** Three players passing between each other, on a signal from the trainer, the player with the puck chooses the 1:1 situation and attacks the goal. The player nearest him defends against him.

**b)** The defending player passes the puck and exerts passive pressure from his position. The player with the puck shoots and skates in the other corner to take up defense there.

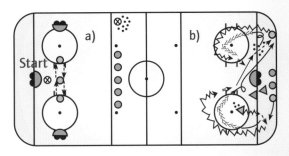

**Exercise 48**

3 x 1:1 situations in a confined space. The defending player acts passively. If the forward loses the puck, he receives a fresh one from the second defender. The exercise is done from both sides at the same time.

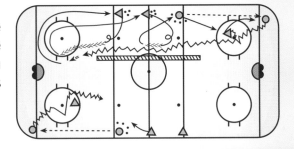

**Exercise 49**

**4 x 1:1:**

**a)** In the corner.

**b)** Two players are each holding two sticks; each tries to pull the other person across.

**c)** Doing a slalom without the puck and after the pass 1:1.

**d)** The defending player passes the puck to the attacking player, both players must remain behind the cone, close-quarter marking is important.

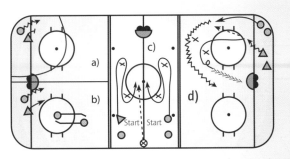

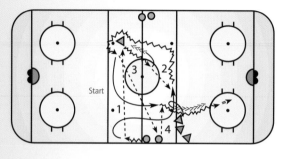

### Exercise 50

1:1, the forward passes the puck diagonally to the defender and sets off towards the blue line. The defender starts off with the puck and passes it back to the forward. The defender then returns skating backwards to his original position. The player with the puck skates round him, exchanges the puck with the other forward and concludes the action with a 1:1 situation against the other defending player.

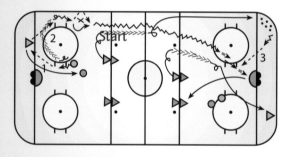

### Exercise 51

1:1: The forward passes the puck to the player behind the goal net and skates backwards in order to be able to take on a pass. He does a turn and skates round a cone and frees himself from the 1:1 situation up to the red line with the first defender. The second defender comes in from the blue line. Shot at goal. The first defender passes the puck in from the corner to the forward to carry out a second shot at goal.

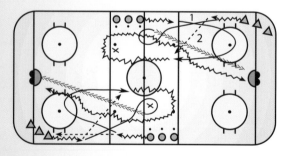

### Exercise 52

1:1: The attacking players start from the neutral zone, and pass the puck to the defending player and go into a curve, ready to take on a pass from the defender and then further as in the Diagram 1:1.

**Exercise 53**

1:1, the attacking players with pucks do a slalom, the defenders without pucks skate in a circle forwards and backwards and after rounding the last cone come into a 1:1 situation.

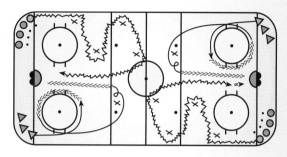

**Exercise 54**

1:1, the forward skates with the puck round the cone, the defending player without the puck changes over from skating forwards to backwards, and then further into a 1:1 situation.

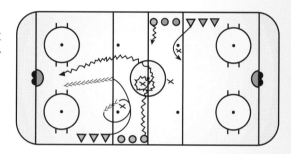

**Exercise 55**

1:1, the attacking player may not start off before he receives the puck, the defending player skates backwards round half of the center circle, 1:1 situation one defender against two forwards, two defenders against one forward, at the conclusion change round of roles.

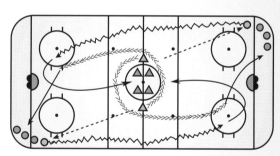

**Exercise 56**

1:1, the players start on a signal, they have to skate round a cone, close marking and making contact with the opponent at the beginning of the 1:1 situation are important.

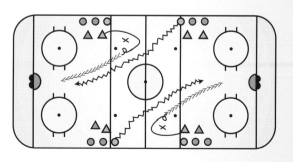

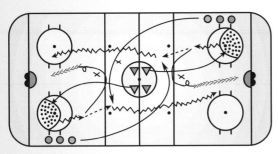

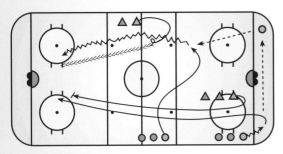

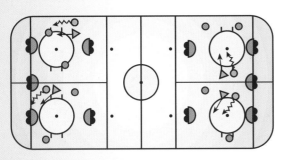

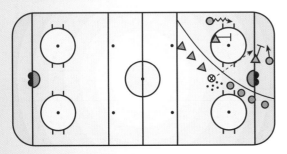

### Exercise 57

1:1, all four players start off without a puck on a signal. The defending player gathers in the puck, passes it to the forward and moves off straight away on the other side, where they skate round the cone and then defend in a 1:1 situation.

### Exercise 58

1:1 + backchecking of the player without the puck. The forward with the puck skates behind the goal net, passes the puck to the trainer and sets off back into the second end zone. The backchecking player marks him by taking up the correct position. The second forward receives the pass from the trainer and plays round the other defending player in a 1:1 situation.

### Exercise 59

1:1. The players are in the end zones in both halves of the ice. Two standing teammates assist the attacking player, who can be passed to. Change round positions after 30 seconds.

### Exercise 60

2:2 in a confined space with man marking. Loading of effort 20 seconds. If necessary, the trainer passes in another puck. On a whistle signal, the players leave the puck lying and leave the ice. At the same time, four more players start the exercise.

## 16.2 Individual Game Play – Requiring Higher Coordination

### Exercise 61
**Puck handling:**

a) In a curve on one leg on the outside edge of the skate.

b) On the inside edge of the skate.

c) Skating, doing snake lines on one leg.

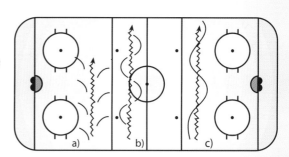

### Exercise 62
**Puck handling:**

a) Turns on one leg.

b) Turning while kneeling down.

c) Turns by jumping from one leg onto the other.

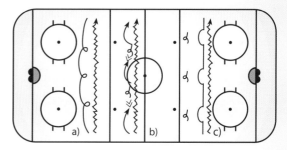

### Exercise 63
**Puck handling:**

a) With agility exercises – sit down – stand up – lie down – stand up.

b) Kicking with alternate legs – "Cossack dance".

c) Puck handling skating forwards and backwards in a square.

d) The puck is moved in a figure of eight in both directions.

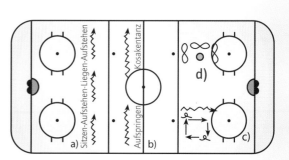

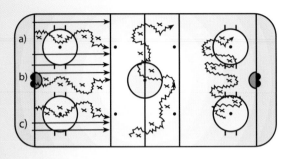

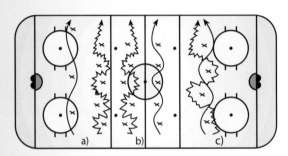

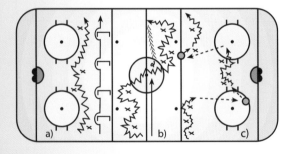

### Exercise 64

**Puck handling and dribbling** – straight lines indicate the path of the skates, snaky lines indicate the path of the puck.

**a)** Puck handling, only the puck goes round the cones (the cones stay in the middle).

**b)** The legs stay on the left of the slalom course.

**c)** The legs stay on the right of the slalom course.

### Exercise 65

**Puck handling and dribbling:**

**a)** The player does a slalom on the one side with the puck going through a slalom course alongside.

**b)** The paths of the player and the puck oscillate against each other as they do the slalom.

**c)** The paths of the player and the puck oscillate against each other as they do the slalom, but this time both run down one single slalom course.

### Exercise 66

**Puck handling and dribbling:**

**a)** Do a slalom with the stick and puck while the player skates alongside jumping over hurdles.

**b)** Do a slalom with the stick and the puck, left and right, forwards and backwards, the legs stay outside the course (the cones remain in the middle).

**c)** Do a slalom with a pass and change over to skating backwards.

## Exercise 67

**a)** Slalom – dribbling two pucks with the stick.

**b)** Slalom – dribbling two pucks, one with the stick and the other with the skate.

**c)** Dribble the second puck with the skate.

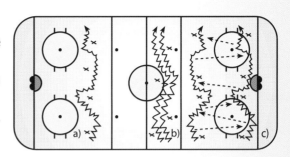

## Exercise 68

**Slalom with the puck:**

**a)** Jumping over little hurdles.

**b)** Jumping over and ducking under (e.g., on the stomach) hurdles.

**c)** Jumping over with turns.

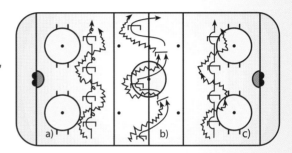

## Exercise 69

**a)** Five players play passing with two pucks between them.

**b)** In pairs – passing, one puck with the stick, the other with the skate.

**c)** In pairs against each other, passing with the stick, always change over, turning from skating forwards to backwards and vice versa.

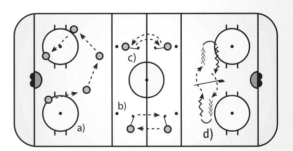

## Exercise 70

**Playing "Piggy in the middle" in a circle, before passing do an agility exercise.**

**a)** Knees bend.

**b)** Kneeling on one knee, on both knees.

**c)** Turns.

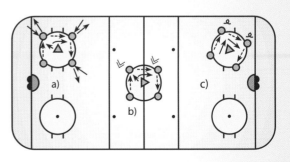

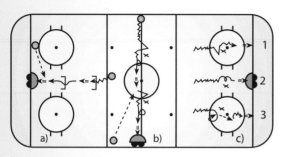

### Exercise 71

**a)** Puck handling, jumping over hurdles, shooting at goal, receiving passes, jumping over hurdles, shot at goal.

**b)** Puck handling, dodges, turn, shoot at goal, receive a pass, dodge, turn, shoot at goal.

**c)** Puck handling – at the last moment the trainer says in which corner of the goal the shot is to be directed.

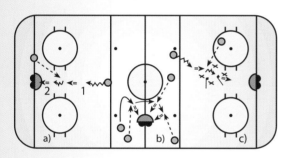

### Exercise 72

**a)** Shots at goal – first shot is at the upper left corner of the net. The second shot in the lower right-hand corner.

**b)** The player starts off towards goal without a puck and receives three passes, one after the other from different directions.

**c)** The player starts off with a puck and shoots at goal, he receives a second puck pass and tries to shoot at goal between the hurdles.

# 16.3    Game Combinations

**Exercise 73**

"Give and go" – the basic exercise.

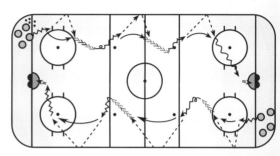

**Exercise 74**

"Give and go". To start with it is better when the trainer does the passing. Emphasis – increase of speed by the player immediately after he has passed.

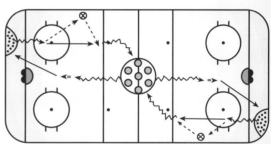

**Exercise 75**

"Give and go". The player doing the passing starts off in the direction where he passes to.

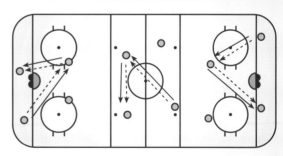

**Exercise 76**

"Give and go". The player starts off rapidly after making the pass in a particular direction.

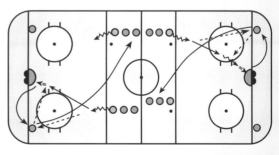

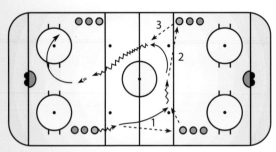

### Exercise 77

"Give and go". During the exercise, the player does 3 passes, after learning the exercise it is done on both sides at the same time.

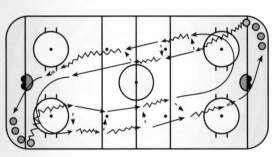

### Exercise 78

"Give and go" is done in a 2:0 situation. The player on the boards must receive a pass before he reaches the blue line. The player, who has done the pass skates on deep into the zone and in a 2:0 situation back again.

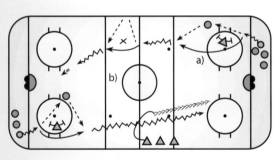

### Exercise 79

"Give and go". This is an exercise for building up the attack in the defense zone with a passive defender opposing.

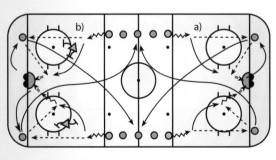

### Exercise 80

"Give and go". Exercise with the emphasis on the combination to conclude the attack.

**a)** Without an opponent.

**b)** With a passive defender opposing.

**Exercise 81**

"Crossing". Basic exercise – for the conclusion it is important that the player not carrying out the shot moves in up to the goal (rebound shot and puck feinting).

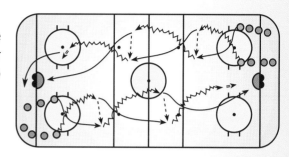

**Exercise 82**

"Crossing and doing a drop pass".
**a)** Each player in a pair skates twice.
**b)** Skate only in one direction.

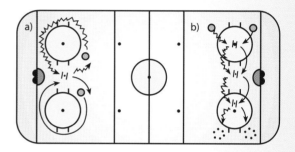

**Exercise 83**

"Crossing and doing a drop pass".

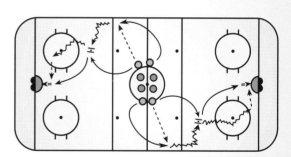

**Exercise 84**

"Crossing and doing a drop pass". This is done twice during the exercise.

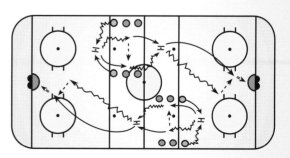

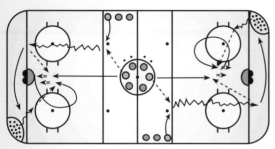

### Exercise 85

"Return pass". The player with the puck in the center face-off circle passes the puck to a second player and afterwards there is a return pass from the goal line. The player making the pass collects a second puck from the corner and passes it to the player to make a shot.

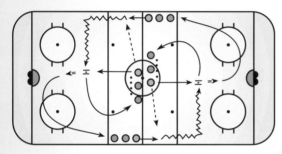

### Exercise 86

"Drop pass". The player passes the puck from the center face-off circle to the player on the boards, who then brings the puck towards the center where he does a drop pass. The player without the puck has to time his movements so that the whole action can be concluded with a shot at goal.

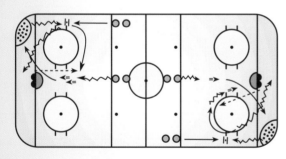

### Exercise 87

"Drop pass and return pass". The player starts off again from the center circle, shoots at goal and then collects another puck from the corner, does a drop pass to another player, who starts off after a little delay. The player with the puck skates behind the goal line and does a return pass.

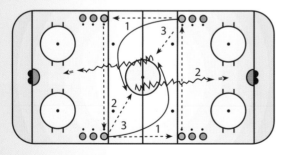

### Exercise 88

"Starting off into a clear area". The player passes the puck and skates round the center face-off circle into a clear area. Here he receives a pass from the group standing opposite. The exercise takes place on both sides of the ice.

**Exercise 89**

"Starting off into a clear area". The defender skates from the center circle backwards and receives a puck pass, turns to skate forwards and passes the puck to the player, who has started off from the area of the boards. At the same time, the player starts from the center circle in a curve into the attacking zone and after a pass shoots at goal. The exercise takes place on both sides of the ice at the same time.

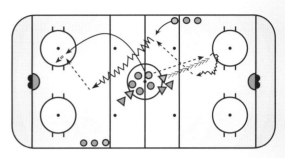

**Exercise 90**

"Starting off into a clear area". The player starts off from the boards, gathers the puck pass and deep in the attacking zone he carries out a feinting movement in the opposite direction and passes the puck to a second player.

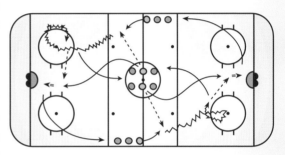

**Exercise 91**

2:1. The game situation is played out in the neutral zone by doing crossing. In the attacking zone it is done using a return pass.

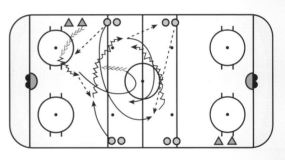

**Exercise 92**

2:1. The attacking player practices crossing in the neutral zone and in the attacking zone, crossing and drop passes. The exercise takes place on both sides of the ice at the same time.

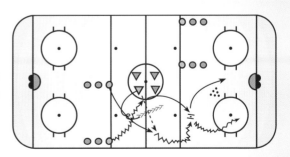

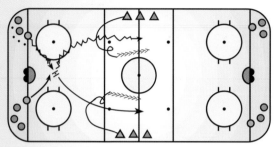

### Exercise 93

"Taking on the opponent". Exercise to practice taking on the opponent against crossing. The player taking the opponent on pushes the forwards towards the boards and always keep themselves in the vicinity of the central axis of the ice.

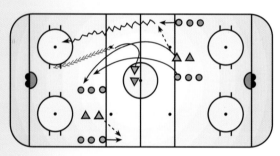

### Exercise 94

"Taking on the opponent". The exercise concentrates on the cooperation of the player taking on the opponent in the neutral zone – the forwards and the defenders skate back.

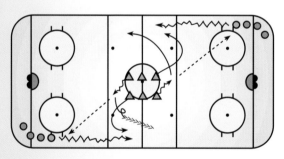

### Exercise 95

"Securing space". The second defender secures space by his movements and positioning for the activities being carried out by the first defender.

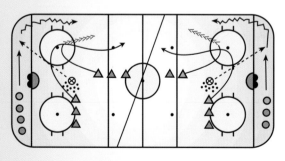

### Exercise 96

"Securing space and taking on the opponent ". The exercise concentrates on cooperation in a defense combination in the attacking zone.

## Exercise 97
"Securing space in the neutral zone".

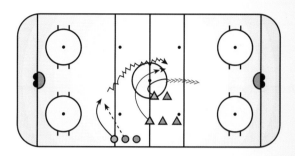

## Exercise 98
"Securing space in the defending zone". The exercise is carried out in both halves of the ice at the same time.

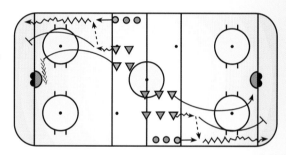

## Exercise 99
"Man marking". The player with the puck plays the puck to the forward from behind the goal net, who then breaks away.

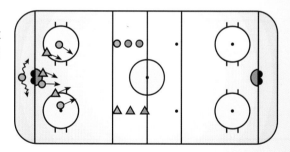

## Exercise 100
"Man marking". The exercise is started by the trainer passing the puck to a forward.

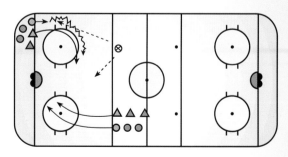

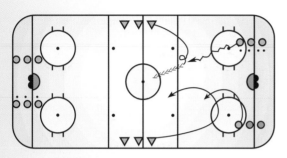

### Exercise 101

"Man marking". The attacking players try to resolve the 2:2 situation using man marking and concluding by shooting at goal.

## 16.4 Cooperation on the Attack

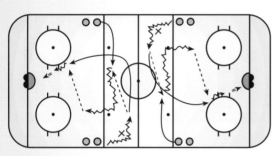

### Exercise 102

2:0. Only a maximum of two passes is allowed to be taken in the attacking zone. The players are forced to shoot at goal quickly.

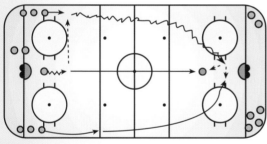

### Exercise 103

3:0. The players must maintain sufficient depth and width in the attack. In the attacking zone, they conclude the action by using the attack triangular formation.

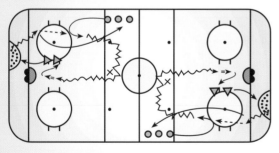

### Exercise 104

Building up the attack in the defense zone, concluding with a 1:0 situation – preparatory exercise. When playing and concluding, the players change round roles. The exercise takes place on both sides of the ice at the same time.

## Exercise 105

Concluding the attack in the defense zone, 2:0 – preparatory exercise. The defender begins with the shot at goal, skates further backwards, receives the puck from the forward and skates behind the goal net. The forward must ensure they start off in good time. The passing player skates into the center, the second forward is on the boards, conclude 2:0.

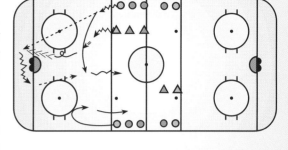

## Exercise 106

Building up the attack in the defending zone – preparatory exercise. One defender begins by doing shots at goal, the second one by skating backwards. Carry on then as in the previous exercise.

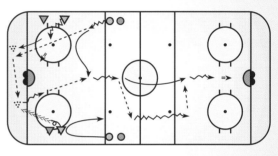

# APPENDIX

## SYMBOLS

| Symbol | Meaning | Symbol | Meaning |
|---|---|---|---|
| ⊗ | Trainer | \| \| \| \| | Skating sideways – this is for the special exercise for the cross-over of the legs – skating sideways with legs crossing |
| ● | Attacking player | | |
| ▲ | Defending player | ∿∿➤ | Skating forwards in puck possession |
| ⟶ | Skating forwards not in puck possession | - - -➤ | Passing |
| ≫≫➤ | Skating backwards | ⟹ | Shooting |
| ⟶ɪ | Stopping | ⊣ | Checking |
| ⟀ | Turning/Turn | ⟜ | Screening/covering/protecting (the puck) |
| | Jumping over an obstacle/hurdle | ∴∴ | Pucks |
| | Ducking under an obstacle/hurdle | O × | Training equipment and aids (cones/stands) |
| ≪ | Kneeling | 7 | Ice hockey stick |
| ↓ | Doing a knees bend | ◗ | Goal |
| ↑ | Jumping up | | |
| ∞ | Circling/Doing a figure of eight | | |

## PHOTO & ILLUSTRATION CREDITS

Cover design:        Jens Vogelsang, Aachen
Cover photo:         dpa Picture-Alliance GmbH, Frankfurt
Internal Photos:     Photos on pages 8, 23, 25, 142, 201 Ales Tvrznik
All other photos:    dpa Picture-Alliance GmbH, Frankfurt
Graphics/Diagrams:   Jana Tvrzniková